FACE PAINTING

FACE
PAINTING

African-American Beauty Techniques from
an Emmy Award–Winning Makeup Artist

REGGIE WELLS
with Theresa Foy DiGeronimo

HENRY HOLT AND COMPANY ～ NEW YORK

Henry Holt and Company, Inc.
Publishers since 1866
115 West 18th Street
New York, New York 10011

Henry Holt® is a registered trademark
of Henry Holt and Company, Inc.

Due to limitations of space, photo credits appear on page 190.

The use of any individual's name or photograph in this book should not
be construed as an endorsement of this book or of the author's services.

Library of Congress Cataloging-in-Publication Data
Wells, Reggie.
Face painting: African-American beauty techniques from an Emmy
Award–winning makeup artist / Reggie Wells with Theresa Foy DiGeronimo.
p.   cm.
ISBN 0-8050-5217-8 (hb: alk. paper)
1. Beauty, Personal. 2. Afro-American women—Health and hygiene.
3. Cosmetics. 4. Beauty culture. 5. Consumer education.
I. DiGeronimo, Theresa Foy.
RA778.4.A36W44   1998
646.7'2—dc21   98-16098

Henry Holt books are available for special promotions
and premiums. For details contact: Director, Special Markets.

First Edition 1998

ILLUSTRATIONS BY KAREN PUGH
DESIGNED BY KELLY SOONG

Printed in the United States of America
All first editions are printed on acid-free paper.∞

1 3 5 7 9 10 8 6 4 2

I dedicate this book to my family:
my parents, John and Ada Wells, who
watched me in my growth and guided me
in my life and allowed me to be who I am;
my brothers, John, Ronald, and Anthony; and
my sisters, Patricia, Pricilla, and Orrie.
I love you all.

I also dedicate this book to my colleagues
and friends who are no longer with us:
Al Grundy, Stanley James, Andre Douglas,
John Kellman Grier, and Michael Weeks.
I will forever miss you.

Contents

Acknowledgments   *ix*

Reggie's Philosophy   *xi*

PART *I*

THE ARTIST BEHIND THE BRUSH   3

PART *II*

SPECIAL CELEBRITY MOMENTS   19

*Leontyne Price • Whitney Houston • Vanessa Williams • Robin Givens •
Patti LaBelle • Naomi Campbell • Anita Baker • Beverly Johnson •
Oprah Winfrey • Iman • Diahann Carroll • Aretha Franklin • Chaka Khan •
Susan L. Taylor • Special Colleagues*

PART *III*

BEAUTY SECRETS *131*

Making the Eyes the Focal Point of the Face • Taming and Shaping Eyebrows • Coloring and Sculpting Lips • Contouring a Full Face • Caring for Your Skin

PART *IV*

BEAUTY MAKEOVERS *165*

Painting the Canvas • Makeover One: Dark Skin • Makeover Two: Medium Skin • Makeover Three: Light Skin

PART V

CLIENT LIST *185*

Acknowledgments

I would like to acknowledge the help of my editors, Tracy Sherrod and Amelia Sheldon, and my agent, Jeff Herman; Wilhelmina for giving me my start; the Zoli Illusion Agency, especially Susan Branagan and Lelia Raibourn, for standing by me for ten years; Ken Barboza, my first agent; and Tony Barboza, my first photographer. I would also like to thank:

Harpo Productions for their support

My favorite makeup artists:
Fran Cooper, Roxanna Floyd, Sam Fine, Eric Spearman, Tony Marshall, and Zianni Coats

Essence magazine:
Susan L. Taylor, editor-in-chief, and Mikki Taylor, cover and beauty editor

The Ink Well

The Maryland Institute College of Art and its alumni staff

My best friends who stood by me and helped me put this book together:
Terrence Sneed, Josephine Johnson, Theresa Thompson, Ozella Barksdale, William Thomas, Ruth Barksdale, and Sheryl Bailey

Warmest thanks to my supporters at Henry Holt and Company:
Wendy Sherman, Lucy Albanese, Kelly Soong, Maggie Richards, Raquel Jaramillo, and Ida Veltri

Reggie's Philosophy

I believe that makeup application shouldn't be a complicated matter. It should be easy and fun. That's why I've tried to simplify the process of applying makeup. I want you to feel confident that you can follow the instructions today—not next month after hours of practice and frustrating mistakes.

I decided to use this simplistic approach because of something I learned as an art teacher. At first, my students came to class with no idea what they were doing—some just let color fly and hoped it would land in the right places; others didn't even try because they insisted they couldn't draw a thing. To help my students gain skill and confidence, I gave them coloring books and told them to practice coloring inside the lines, paying attention to shape and structure.

The pictures in these books were very simple line drawings that gave them the opportunity to concentrate on the basics of art. Once the students grasped the concepts of shape, color, shading, highlighting, and blending within the lines, they were ready to take these basic skills and experiment creatively; they were eager to go to a blank canvas and artistically and skillfully express themselves.

Applying makeup is very much like painting. Without training, most women just let the color land where it may, or they feel intimidated and don't try much at all. The results detract from their natural beauty rather than enhance it. This book is your coloring book. Here you'll learn an easy approach to coloring inside the lines. I tell you the colors to use and where to place each color; I give you basic techniques for blending and highlighting. Once you understand these fundamentals, you'll have the skills you need to explore and experiment further on the canvas of your face.

I think it's very important to start simple. When I started out in makeup, I read many books that confused rather than helped me. The directions were so complicated, and the authors talked too much about what *they* do to create a certain effect—not what the reader could do at home. I've also noticed that makeup books that are very detailed become quickly outdated because makeup styles and applications change over time. I had just about given up looking for help in makeup books when I found a treasure. It was a book by Way Bandy, a makeup artist in the 1970s. This book was very clear and simple. It told me exactly what color to use and where to put it. I've tried to write my book with the same kind of easy instructions you can follow without feeling intimidated or confused. The illustrations are large and simple, to show you the correct placement of color and to give you the confidence you need to believe that you can do it yourself. These makeup lessons won't show you how to follow the fads of today or how to be on the edge of style. They are intended to show you how makeup can be applied to make you look your best at any time, in any year, and for any occasion. By explaining the basics of makeup application, this book will be as valuable to you in the year 2010 as it is today.

ᕦ

I believe everyone is creative—but few realize they can use their creativity to enhance their natural beauty. Do you find an outlet for your creative side in cooking or decorating or crafts? Are you involved in carpentry or music or drama? All of these things give life to the artist who exists inside us. Now let that artist create with your makeup. Don't let yourself get stuck in one particular look because you don't know what else to do. Experiment! Use this book as your guide to exploring and enjoying color. If you have added a decorator's touch to your home or tried a new recipe in the last year but haven't added a single new color to your makeup box, then it's definitely time to get a new paint box of colors and challenge that artist within.

I'm not suggesting that you drop all the makeup habits you've developed over the years. I don't want you to give up makeup techniques that you believe work for you. I'm suggesting only that you give yourself the freedom to try something new. Start slowly if you like. If you just love the lipstick color you wear now and don't want to change it—fine, keep it. But why not try a new eye shadow using a color off the color chart? Or try a new foundation and use the double-foundation technique to blend the uneven skin tones? Wear it for a few days and see how you feel. I'm not telling you to throw away everything you've ever done and start all over again. I just want to encourage you to see yourself as an artist who can use color to create beauty.

I believe that celebrities are regular people just like you and me. I've included their stories in this book to show you that their makeup problems and concerns are the same as yours. One was afraid to try a new look; some needed to condition their skin before they could apply makeup at all; others were stuck in old colors and styles; one was brave enough to try a bold new lip color but then decided it wasn't for her. Some know exactly what they want; others try

something new all the time. See . . . just like you. When I work with a celebrity, her skin is no different than any other woman's. She brings to me a canvas that needs painting. That's what makeup is all about—it lets *all* women look and feel glamorous.

I believe that African-American women have the natural beauty advantage. Mother Nature has primed your skin to welcome color application. The African-American canvas comes in a whole range of dark tones, each primed for a different spectrum on the color wheel. This innate ability to accept and wear color is part of our heritage. Our forebears have shown us that it is in color, dance, music, painting, and song that we celebrate our life.

Face Painting

PART I

THE
ARTIST
BEHIND
THE BRUSH

I believe that no matter how many false directions we may be pulled in during our lives, eventually we end up in the place where we belong. My journey to this place where I now stand and know I belong began back in Baltimore.

I was the third born in a family of seven children. I remember that I was in the second grade when I discovered my drawings were better than my classmates'. Mine had more detail, more depth, more color. Just as some children might run home with their good classwork papers, I ran home with my drawings—full of pride and enthusiasm. But to my parents, John and Ada, they were no more than simple pictures that didn't warrant a second look (or even a revered place on the refrigerator). I learned to accept that although I thought my work was exceptional, it was really nothing to get excited about.

That was until I met Mrs. Mintz. She owned the grocery store in our neighborhood where I got a job when I was about eight years old. A widow with three boys of her own, Mrs. Mintz let me earn some money by stocking the shelves, organizing the produce, and cleaning up a bit. When things were slow, I would doodle and draw. Mrs. Mintz noticed and asked me lots of questions about what I was drawing and how I created my pictures. She was the first person to take an interest in this talent and to encourage me to let it out.

I continued working for Mrs. Mintz until I graduated from high school, which is probably the only reason I ended up in college. Knowing that education would be important for whatever direction I chose to take my talent, Mrs. Mintz bought my high school ring for me on the condition that I finish high school and apply to college. After that she was always asking me to draw for her, and then she'd quiz me on what I did in school and what I was doing to make sure I'd get into college. It was this guardian angel who took me under her wing and challenged me to practice my art, to push my talent to the edge, to do something with it that I would love for the rest of my life.

My parents loved me and wanted the best for me, but with six other children to care for, they didn't have the time or the know-how to concentrate on just one child who needed encouragement. Mrs. Mintz stepped in and took over that role. (Maybe there really is a special quality that belongs to Jewish mothers alone.) She made me feel special, and sometimes that feeling is enough to carry any child toward any dream.

The dream seemed close to becoming a reality when I earned a scholarship to the Maryland Institute College of Art, where I planned to study fashion design. My loves were drawing and painting, and I was excited by the idea that I could combine these with my love for fashion. I went off to school thinking I had a straightforward path to follow, but soon I faced an unexpected curve. Without someone like Mrs. Mintz to help me keep my goals in sight, I was turned around in a different direction. I was told by the school counselor that I had a slim-to-none chance of making a living as a black fashion designer—she believed that the world just wasn't ready for African-American designers. She insisted that art education was the best route to take. I certainly didn't want to put in four years of study to find out that the fashion world had no place for me, so I switched my major to a field that could offer me a job upon graduation.

I took my first job teaching at an inner-city junior high school in Baltimore. I liked classroom teaching, but I needed to do something more creative, more artistic, more fashion oriented. Good teaching, I knew, must include exposing students to new things and letting them apply the knowledge they gain in the classroom to the world in which they live. So I started a modeling and grooming club where I taught girls how to look good, how to dress, how to wear makeup, and how to do their hair. Because I loved doing it and the girls could feel this, the club became very popular. Eventually, it grew into

a theater-dance workshop. I had a background in tap, modern dance, and ballet, and so it was fun to combine these talents with the fashion and flair of theater. In addition to my scheduled art classes, I worked with more than five art- and fashion-related clubs for the next six years. Because I had created someplace to vent my love of "showbiz" and fashion, I felt good about myself—but I became even more convinced that I was in the wrong place.

I realized that it was too late for me to get into fashion designing, but maybe there was a way into the fashion industry through some other door. The girls in my club really liked the way I used makeup to make them look glamorous. They were always after me to do their faces up and show them how to do it themselves. Then I started doing makeup for three of my friends. My cousin Ruthie, neighborhood friend Vivian, and college friend Theresa let me experiment on them. They sat patiently as I tried techniques and ideas that sometimes made them look beautiful and other times made them look silly. But they were good friends and always encouraged me to try again. After a while they all declared that I was really good and should do makeup profes-

sionally. So I began freelancing at a local hair salon doing makeup for women. Again and again everyone said I was good enough to work in New York. I didn't really know what that meant, but it planted the seed of an idea. Maybe I should go to New York.

In 1979 I went. With no real money, no idea if I could get a job, and nowhere to stay, I went. I called some friends who had moved to New York and asked if I

could stay with them until I found a job. I brought with me what I thought was a surefire portfolio of my work—it was a small black book containing enlarged Polaroid shots of my three friends wearing makeup I'd applied. But when I got to New York, I found out that the salons in the city wouldn't hire me without what they considered professional experience—schoolgirls, friends, and a few ladies in a Baltimore beauty salon didn't count.

If I couldn't apply makeup, what else could I do? I had to think of something quick if I wanted to stay in New York. I got a job selling makeup in department stores. This was a low time for me. I didn't want to sell makeup— I wanted to apply it, create with it, make women beautiful with it. Fortunately, selling makeup wasn't the dead end I worried it might be. I found out that the makeup manufacturers hired freelance people to do makeovers right at the store counter in the hopes of selling makeup. This was for me!

First I got a job with Jerome Alexander Co. doing makeovers to sell makeup brushes. Then I moved on to Halston, Calvin Klein, Revlon, Stagelight Cosmetics, Christian Dior, and Chanel. I could make $85 a day freelancing with any one of these companies—which sounded great at first, but because the work wasn't steady (sometimes just one job in two weeks), I still found it very hard to stay alive. After about two years of this I was ready to give up. I had a college degree; I should be able to make a living. I told myself it was time to go back home and try teaching again. Creatively I was getting very good at makeup application, but it wasn't paying the bills. Then something happened that showed me why I could never give up on my dream.

I was doing the makeup of a young model one day at a department store. She told me about a thousand-dollar-a-plate benefit fashion show that was going to take place at Saks Fifth Avenue that night. How I wished I could be one of the makeup artists at that kind of event. Well, knowing that wishing wasn't going to make it happen, I gathered together all the New York nerve and bravado I could muster and headed over to Saks that night after work. With my makeup kit in hand, I went around to the back door and walked in. I was stopped by a security guard who gave me directions to the models' dressing area when I showed him my kit and said I was a makeup artist. I didn't even need to lie—I *was* a makeup artist!

The next thing I knew I was in the middle of the wonderful chaos that lives backstage at any fashion show. As soon as I walked in I heard a model on the left saying, "I need lipstick." Another one against the right wall was calling out for translucent powder. In the swirl of confusion women were pleading with me to do their makeup, so I started right in. In a moment of déjà vu, I thought of the excitement before our fashion shows at school, of the girls all clamoring for my help. Now as I looked around, I saw really big-name models like Iman and Kim Alexis and knew this was the real thing. The rush. The charge. The excitement. The glamour. This was where I wanted to be. I knew there was no turning back now.

The next morning I was at the department store counter again, but with revived enthusiasm. I knew where I was headed, and I knew I belonged. (The night before, a few people had asked for my name and number and promised to call to book me for work—my hopes were soaring high!) This renewed drive showed in my work, and soon I was building a following. Customers were starting to follow me from job to job as I went from Bloomingdale's, to Saks, to Neiman Marcus, to Lord & Taylor. This brought me a lot of attention on my job. Once I was doing a makeover and talking all the time about what I was doing and why I was doing it, and what I was using to create the different effects. I looked up and found I had drawn quite a crowd. Finally my years as a teacher were paying off—I felt very comfortable talking and teaching while I put on the makeup. I realized this was a great way to draw in customers and sell more products.

Women liked that I talked to them and offered to teach them how to take care of their skin and apply makeup. I got so good at it, I actually got into trouble at one of the stores. I was selling Halston products in the same counter area as other promotional makeup artists for other companies. I was called off the floor by the cosmetics supervisor and told to stop talking so loudly while I was doing my makeovers—the other makeup artists were complaining that they couldn't get any business because I was taking all the customers. "Makeup artists at department store counters," she said, "aren't supposed to do so much talking and demonstrating." I closed my mouth and continued working.

Fortunately for me, just a short time after that a young model came in for a makeover. She liked my work, and when I finished she asked for my name and number. It turned out that she had a boyfriend who was a photographer she wanted me to meet. We arranged to meet at his studio, and I did this girl's makeup for a test shot. When the photographer saw the results, he hired me on the spot for a big job he had coming up. "It pays $750," he said. "What do you mean?" I managed to get out. "$750 a week? A month? A what?" It was $750 a day! The shoot was part of a start-up campaign for a new product—Jordache jeans—and the money was great. The teaching job I was thinking of going back to paid $8,000 for a whole year. Well, forget that. Now I could make real money doing what I loved. Finally I saw where I fit. I have to say, it was this photographer, Hank Londoner, who gave me my start in the business.

Londoner gave me lots more work after this first job, and I was able to put together an impressive portfolio. I took my book to an agency and was immediately signed on. One job led to another, and soon I was working with big-name models like Kim Alexis, Carol Alt, and Janice Dickenson, making more and more money as my rates went up to a thousand dollars a day for ads with Revlon, Avon, and Almay.

With this reputation to take with me, I decided I'd like to work with the models at *Essence* magazine. In 1983 I made an appointment to see the editor in chief, Susan L. Taylor. She skimmed through my portfolio and quickly told me that I wasn't

Ce Soir

Say it without a word.

prepared to work with her models; I had only two shots of African-American women in the whole book. "Your book is very good and very strong," she said, "but the majority of your work has been with white women. I need to see your work with black models before I can take you on." Although I was disappointed, I was also encouraged because Ms. Taylor didn't reject me cold; she told me to come back when I had more experience with black women. This gave me a new goal.

It was time to return to the place where I'd started. All my work in Baltimore was on black women, and I loved doing their faces. The idea of working with black women once again excited me. I offered black women something they'd never had before—makeup blended specifically for their skin.

At the time most makeup was formulated for white skin. My artistic background taught me how to mix and blend the colors to make them work on dark skin. Working with an artist's palette, I came up with things that weren't even on the market. They couldn't get this in a bottle; there was a whole ethnic population of women who needed me.

From that point on I sought out African-American models and asked to be sent on jobs with black women. There was an agency called Wilhelmina that worked with young black models. Wilhelmina let me do a lot of her test work for her girls. This helped me quickly build up a strong portfolio of black makeup examples. About eight months later, I returned to *Essence* with this new book. Ms. Taylor was now impressed. She hired me on the spot for the next day. And so I began working right away with beautiful women such as Stephanie Mills, Melba Moore, Anita Baker, and Vanessa Williams. Once I

had done their makeup for the *Essence* shoot, these women liked what they saw and often would ask me to do their makeup on other jobs. From that I became known as one of the leading makeup artists for black models. Being black myself made me a novelty in the business—this wasn't the bad thing my counselor had predicted; it put me in great demand.

Now here I am, where my heart told me I belonged—not in fashion design, where I first envisioned myself—but in makeup, where I can design faces and create glamour. Naturally, I love to work with the world's most beautiful women, but I also love the freedom it gives me to be artistic and creative, and to be true to myself.

This tenacious belief that I belonged in the business has brought me rewards I could never have asked for. I have applied makeup on the cover models of sixty-five *Essence* magazines. I've applied the makeup on African-American women in issues of *Glamour*, *Mademoiselle*, *Bazaar*, *Life*, *Time*, and *Bride's* magazines. I've demonstrated the attractive effect of manufacturers' products in print ads for Maybelline, Avon, Fashion Flair, and Almay. I've also

worked on television studio sets preparing models for their appearances in many commercials, including some for Hanes, Fashion Flair, Soft Sheen, and Avon. I have served as makeup consultant for this country's leading manufacturers of skin-care lines for women of color. I have been asked to create new color lines and discuss principles and strategies for companies such as Mary Kay, Arbonne International, Posner, Black Opal, and Avon. In 1989, I took up residence on the set of *The Oprah Winfrey Show*. During my six years with Oprah, I received three Emmy nominations for daytime television makeup artist; and I won the award in 1995!

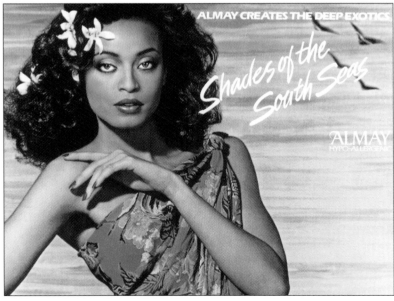

Today my client list reads like a who's who among African-American celebrities. My female and male clients have taken me on a long and winding road to get to where I am today. It was a journey filled with disappointments, setbacks, and frustration, but also with determination, some luck, and lots of joy. All of this has brought me here to where I belong—to the place Mrs. Mintz encouraged me to go.

My last meeting with this wonderful woman was on Thanksgiving Day 1991. After a long separation, I spent the holiday with her at her son's home in Baltimore. It was the most appropriate occasion for me to thank her for all she had done to help me reach my goals (goals I didn't even know I had back in that old grocery store). This day became even dearer to me when Mrs. Mintz died less than a year later. Our last meeting was like the completion of a journey: from the point of the first step to the point of accomplishment. She had shown me the direction, and I eventually found the way.

In this book I'm very happy to share with you stories that highlight the fun I've had along the way. I've detailed the experiences I've had working with some of these glamorous celebrities and included a few of their personal makeup tips. I've also given detailed instructions, guidelines, and skin-care and makeup information to help you create the personal image that will make you feel great about yourself every day. When that happens, I will have accomplished one more of my goals—I will have helped you feel pride in the beauty and glamour of your ethnic heritage.

Read and enjoy.

PART II

SPECIAL
CELEBRITY
MOMENTS

LONDON ffrr

OS26660

LEONTYNE
PRICE
SINGS VERDI

AIDA · OTELLO · ERNANI
UN BALLO IN MASCHERA

ISRAEL PHILHARMONIC
ORCHESTRA

ZUBIN
MEHTA

LEONTYNE PRICE

I t was 1981, and I was walking down Seventh Avenue in New York City by Carnegie Hall when I saw it—there up ahead. It was a five-foot-tall billboard for the Grammy-winning album *Leontyne Price Sings Verdi* that launched my professional career as a makeup artist. My work, my makeup, my heart and soul were there for all of New York City to see. What a way to break into the business!

Only a few months earlier I had left my job working the makeup counters in department stores. I put together a portfolio of my work and decided to shop it around. I took my book and went door-to-door to advertising agencies, magazine publishers, and record producers. My most promising meeting was with an art director at RCA. He took time to look through my book carefully and commented that I showed very promising talent in my work with African-American women. But, unfortunately, he didn't need a makeup artist. I left feeling that someday I'd hear from him again.

Only two days later he called to offer me a job. He said that the makeup artist assigned to an album cover shoot was not able to make it. He wanted to know if I could be downtown in two hours. Heck, I thought, if I could fly I would be there in two minutes. I remember feeling the thrill of adrenaline rushing through my body—my first professional job! Then I remember feeling

that adrenaline freeze in my veins when he told me that my first client would be Leontyne Price. *The* Leontyne Price? The first black American to achieve international operatic superstardom, Leontyne Price? She was an all-time favorite of mine. Everything I knew about her buzzed in my head—her Negro spirituals, pop tunes, Christmas carols, hymns, American, French, and German art songs, and the sound of her majestic voice singing complete operas by Bizet, Mozart, Puccini, and Verdi. The same person who had won over a dozen Grammy awards and had performed at the White House was going to be my first client!

Still feeling numb, I quickly dressed and threw my makeup into the box. Funny the things you remember: Even though I was in a pressing hurry, I spent a few minutes running around in circles trying to decide if I should bring false lashes or not. Finally, with all my stuff together, I jumped on the train and rushed from my place in Harlem to downtown Manhattan. I got to the studio within an hour of the phone call.

The photographer was expecting me. I was familiar with his work because he had done a lot of dance magazine covers. He also did a lot of work with opera stars and orchestra conductors. I mentioned that I especially liked the portrait he had done of Zubin Mehta. I kept chattering on about his work, hoping to keep the conversation away from my own background. I was sure he wouldn't be impressed that I had done Mrs. Jones's makeup at the department store counter. I didn't have any credentials, never mind ones that could match his. Thankfully, he ended the conversation with a quick mention that I had come highly recommended by the art director and he was happy to be working this job with me.

About an hour later, Leontyne Price's limousine pulled up in front of the studio. Her manager came inside first and introduced himself. He explained that Ms. Price (and *please* don't call her "Leontyne," he quickly instructed) was about to enter. Her entrance was as grand as any on the stage of the

Metropolitan Opera House. She carried her impressive five-foot-six-inch frame across the threshold of the studio with the same grace and dignity that so often thrilled thousands across the footlights. She was dressed in a full-length, empire-waist gown of deep aqua chiffon that billowed around her ankles as if fluffed by an invisible fan. Topping her regal stature, her hair was wrapped in the kind of turban that had become her signature. (I found out later that Ms. Price always comes to her New York photo shoots fully dressed. She lives in the city and finds it easier and more comfortable to dress in her own home.) As we were introduced, Ms. Price held out her hand to me—I didn't know whether to shake it or kiss it. What does one do in the presence of such talent and beauty?

The relationship between the makeup artist and his client is immediately a close one. Each can feel the mood of the other. Ms. Price, I'm sure, felt my nervousness as I touched her face and rubbed my fingers over her skin. She began to question me about my work and my experience. I hesitated for a moment and then admitted that this was my first time doing a professional album cover. Luckily, she had already been assured that I had done great work on black women. As I began to stammer, she stopped me, and in her naturally melodic voice that combines the Southern drawl of her native Mississippi with a touch of England, she told me, "I am an artist in what I do on the stage. You are an artist in what you do—you paint faces. Today, I am your canvas; on me you will create one of the most successful masterpieces of your career." At that

moment, I wasn't sure if this advice would help me or make me more nervous. But I did listen to her and did feel more comfortable knowing that she respected me as an artist.

As I began, I repeated her words over and over to myself. She had offered me an artistic challenge that I was excited to take on. I now saw her face in ways that I wouldn't have before. I saw that she had very good skin that was as even-toned and clear as the range and color of her voice. This gave me a wonderful canvas to work with. She also had a lot of area around her eyes that gave me plenty of room for painting, sculpting, and

developing. She had wonderfully full lips that balanced her face. I saw that she could wear a lot of different colors with her medium skin tone and superbly theatrical face that helped her carry off the very dramatic look that she often needed onstage.

Not only did I paint, I created. I experienced an inner surge of creativity; I don't know if it came from this boost to my confidence, or from a spiritual base, or from the mere presence of this great diva, but I found myself immersed in my artistry, creating on the blank canvas of her face.

It was easy to hold on to this mind-set because of the way Ms. Price creates a peaceful and calm atmosphere as she sits during her makeup sessions. During this time, all women reveal a lot about their moods and inner self. Some are chatty; others are anxious and find it hard to sit still for long periods. Some conduct business, talk on the phone, give interviews, and find many ways to express their energy. Ms. Price used this time to sit back, close her eyes, relax, and find an inner core of tranquillity. This feeling was contagious, and soon I too felt calm. When I was finished, I was not surprised to find that this was a session that would remain one of the highlights of my career.

After this fabulous first professional experience, I became more confident about my work, and my celebrity client list began to grow. But I always had time for Leontyne Price. I remember we flew to Boston and I did her makeup before her performance with the Boston Pops, and I did the same for her appearance with the Los Angeles Symphony. We also did a few more photo sessions for album covers (a total of four!) and several magazine shots.

It was in Boston that I found out the hard way that Leontyne Price couldn't stand to be around people who wore cologne. As I entered her dressing room, she immediately pulled back sharply as if she had been stung by a bee. She sniffed a bit in my direction and then asked me to leave the room and wash off the cologne. I later learned that Ms. Price is sensitive to perfumed scents and flowers because they can affect the health of her lungs and vocal cords. There

was one saving grace to that night—I was glad I hadn't sent her fragrant flowers as I had planned!

There were so many moments of joy with Ms. Price. How much fun it was during a shoot for *Harper's Bazaar* when Francesco Scavullo, the photographer, filled the room with a recording of Ms. Price singing Verdi's *Aida*. Suddenly, she surprised us all by joining in; she sang her "duet" in a full voice that resonated throughout the studio. The photograph that eventually appeared in the magazines showing Ms. Price with a glorious, full, open-mouthed smile was taken during this impromptu performance. Every time I look at this shot, I can feel the joy that filled the room at that moment.

As I stood looking up at the photo of Ms. Price on her album on the billboard outside Carnegie Hall, I knew I was at a turning point in my career. At that moment, I knew I could make it in this business. I knew that I had the ability to bring out the absolutely gorgeous natural beauty of all women.

WHITNEY HOUSTON

Who is that girl?" I asked myself over and over. I knew I had seen her somewhere before, but I just couldn't place her. She was tall (about five feet eight inches) and about twenty-two years old; she was slender with beautiful, long black hair and brown eyes that sparkled. She was also shy and averted her eyes when she saw me looking at her. I couldn't help but look—she was so beautiful. "Who is she?" I had seen her several times now on this commuter train. We lived near each other in Woodbridge, New Jersey. We both worked in New York. I was doing freelance makeup jobs, but what did she do? What kind of job would such a glamorous young girl have? Then it hit me. Of course, I had seen her in *Seventeen* magazine—she was a model. If only I could catch her eye and start up a conversation, I thought. I'd love to do this girl's makeup. But then the train stopped, she rushed off into the crowd, and I missed my chance.

About a year later, in 1985, I was asked to do a job for *Essence*. It was for a holiday makeup story on a young, up-and-coming vocalist. I had never heard of her, but I guessed she must have something special because we were also going to do a cover try for an issue that would come out after the release of her first album, called *Whitney Houston*.

When I walked into the dressing room, Whitney spun around in her chair to face me. It didn't take me a second to place that face. "I know you," I laughed. "You live in Woodbridge, New Jersey, and sometimes take the train into New York!" "How do you know that?" she asked, looking surprised with those big brown eyes opened wide. "Because I live in the housing complex near you, and I'm the guy who saw you on the train and knew I wanted to work with you," I confessed. Well, Whitney didn't recognize me or know that she'd had a secret admirer, but here we were, finally together, and I couldn't wait to work with that beautiful face.

None of us in the dressing room had ever heard Whitney Houston sing, so we began polite conversation by asking about her new album. We asked her what kind of music she sang, what were the names of some of the songs, and things like that. In her soft-spoken way, Whitney answered our questions and then offered to give us a preview—she had brought a tape of the album. When she popped that cassette into the little tape player sitting on the makeup counter, we all stopped short. Could that strong and confident voice crooning the melodic pop ballad "Saving All My Love for You" really have come from this small-framed girl with the beautiful smile? I was amazed and speechless. When I recovered my voice, the first thing I said was, "You are going to be a star." Well, as time showed, that turned out to be an understatement. The album sold six million in the United States (a record for an album by a black female vocalist) and 10 million worldwide. Four of the singles from the album became top-ten sellers, and our favorite, "Saving All My Love for You," won Whitney the Grammy for best female pop vocalist.

While listening to this music in the studio, I began to examine Whitney's facial features. Her skin was clear—in perfect condition. It's always a pleasure to work on skin that can take the makeup well. I could see that she had one of the prettiest smiles in the business, so I decided that all I had to do was bring out the eyes and let her smile bring out her cheekbones and natural radiance, and half the work would be done already.

With Whitney, less is better. I felt strongly that she would look her best with just a little makeup. Over the years some makeup artists have made the mistake of overpainting Whitney Houston, but I think that anyone who works with her for any length of time soon finds out that her skin tends to look better with less makeup. For a while she got caught up in dark eyes and an overly dramatic accent on her makeup. But now in her motion picture career I see her look is clean, like when we started out together. I would have to guess that Whitney has learned that with her strong, beautiful features, she doesn't need to be overdone.

For that first job, I did three makeup applications on Whitney for a feature story demonstrating different looks for the holiday season. This piece was to show black women how they could use makeup colors to create different effects. On one I used soft browns and golds; on another, pinks and purples and blues. For a very dramatic evening look I brought out Whitney's deep-set eyes. This took Whitney's holiday look from casual day to formal evening.

The story and photos ran in *Essence*, but we were all disappointed when she wasn't chosen for the cover. I believed that Whitney and I and the magazine had all lost out on a big opportunity. I felt for Whitney because, naturally, she wanted to land her first magazine cover. I also believed that she was going to be a big star. I was disappointed for myself because I wanted to be the first to do her makeup for a national cover. But putting this disappointment aside, something good did come out of the experience—I made a friend.

Whitney booked me for many jobs after that. As we got to know each other better, I was thrilled to watch her career take off and to know that she still remained one of the nicest young people in this business. What was especially nice for me was that now, instead of my watching her from a distance on the train, she would give me a ride home from the city in her Mercedes convertible sports car when our schedules allowed. During these "off-duty" rides I learned about her family and her early life. She was always telling me stories about her mother, Emily (better known as Cissy), who was a veteran gospel and R&B singer; she sang backup for many recording artists, including her own niece, Dionne Warwick, and family friend Aretha Franklin. It was Whitney's mother who coached her singing voice during her teen years and who brought her along to sing in clubs and recording studios. At the same time Whitney was getting a taste of showbiz by modeling, and had made a hit in magazines like *Vogue*, *Seventeen*, and *Cosmopolitan*.

As I got to know Whitney a little better, I learned that although she was young and carefree, she knew exactly what she wanted. As she is with her music, Whitney is a perfectionist with her appearance. She knew exactly what she wanted to look like, and she wanted to be knowledgeable about how to create that look. She was always asking me questions like "What's the difference between print and performance makeup?" and "Where do you get that kind of foundation?" "Why are you mixing those colors?" and "What's the name of that color?" She wanted to learn about everything.

I was learning too. I remember one night she wanted me to do her makeup for a live concert in upstate New York. To this point I had worked with her only on still shots like the ones we did for *Essence*, *Glamour*, and *Harper's Bazaar*, never at a performance. I was excited about having this opportunity and looked forward to the challenge. Backstage I was introduced to her family, who (I realized very quickly) were the backbone of her career. Her father was her business manager, her older brother Gary Garland was her backstage

manager, and her other brother, Michael, was her road manager. Her mother was there too to keep everybody else organized. The Houston family all worked together to make it happen.

When Whitney performed, I was amazed. I had never seen so much energy come from one person. This beautiful young lady, who never dropped a bead of sweat during photo sessions, was almost immediately covered with perspiration. She put so much of herself into her songs, both physically and emotionally, that she didn't have to move or dance to perspire; it happened even as she stood singing a ballad. I knew immediately that I was going to have to change the way I applied her makeup. When a person sweats like that, you should use very little or no liquid makeup (it can't withstand profuse stage sweating). Instead, stage performers use a lot of powder, which is more likely to stay on the skin and withstand the sweating. It's also important not to put extreme amounts of eye shadow on someone like Whitney because the color tends to run down the face. I soon learned that with the right amount of makeup Whitney could freshen up between sets by simply patting her face with a dry towel.

Through our years together, I've watched that humble choirgirl grow into a box office blockbuster. We've both moved on, and we've both found our place in this business. Still, I have one regret. Whitney has appeared on two or three covers for *Essence,* and I've done the makeup for women appearing on more than sixty-five *Essence* covers myself. But one of my biggest career disappointments is that we've never done one together. I did do many other magazine shots with her, but never a cover, and that's something I always wanted to do. I'm not resigned to this disappointment, though. If there's one thing I've learned in this business it's this: You never know what lies ahead! I'm expecting that sometime in the future our paths will cross again, and we'll do that magazine cover together.

ESSENCE

Love

The Truth About Marriage: Men and Women Speak Out

Tribute to Willi Smith

New

for Summer— Hair, Makeup, Accessories

Keeping Our Families Strong

Great Food for a Crowd

Plus

New Fiction by Celebrated Author John A. Williams

Vanessa Williams in Love

"Nothing can break us apart"

VANESSA WILLIAMS

I dialed as fast as my fingers could race over the numbers on the phone. I couldn't believe what I had just seen, but there was no time to wonder over it. The most sleek, gifted, intelligent, and breathtakingly beautiful black woman had just been crowned Miss America 1984, and there was no time to waste. The beauty editor at *Essence* magazine answered the phone and immediately agreed with me that, whatever it took, *Essence* had to be the first national magazine to have this girl on the cover. "Oh, one more thing," I added. "I want to do her makeup."

Of course this girl was Vanessa Williams. Like most Americans, the first time I saw her was on television that night of the Miss America pageant. She won me over with her confident and proud style and her outstanding rendition of the Broadway tune "Happy Days Are Here Again" (an old-time favorite of mine). As time would tell, her talent and personality weren't manufactured for this one event; they were the core and soul of this remarkable young woman.

Vanessa did come to New York shortly after the pageant for an *Essence* cover shoot. Because she was rushed in and out so quickly, I wasn't there to do her makeup. But knowing this girl would go far, I had no doubt we'd catch up with each other some other time somewhere down the road.

We met professionally a short time later during a print shoot for another magazine. I noticed right away that she was as confident and pretty in person as she was in public appearances. Her catlike green eyes, her tawny complexion, and her dazzling smile all came together to create an absolutely beautiful face—with one small flaw. Right away, I told her that when I saw her onstage at the Miss America pageant I loved everything about her, but there was one thing that bothered me about her appearance. "All through the performance," I said, "I couldn't stop thinking that you needed your eyebrows tweezed." Vanessa laughed at my candid observation, but it was true. There was too much brow for the face. So that day, I tweezed Vanessa's eyebrows down to a more complementary shape. She saw the difference right away and loved it.

While working with this beautiful face, I wondered, What's this woman really like on the inside? The conversation started with the usual pleasantries: How are you today? Congratulations on being crowned Miss America. And so on. But when I asked her about her choice of song for the talent competition, her face lit up and the conversation took off. Vanessa told me she had been a musical theater major at Syracuse University and absolutely loved Broadway. That was her ambition, she told me, to star in a Broadway play.

What a delight to talk at length to someone so young and yet so knowledgeable about musical theater. And what a thrill to work with someone who was so sure of where she wanted to go and what she wanted to do. Vanessa had it all mapped out. She knew she wanted to record an album, win a Grammy, and go on Broadway and star in her own show. These weren't just the idle dreams of a starstruck girl; they were the calculated and firm goals of a determined and talented young lady. Vanessa believed she could reach out and grab all these things—nothing was impossible for her.

The next time I worked with Vanessa was in her apartment before her appearance on *Good Morning America*. She was getting ready to face her public for the first time since the news leaked that she was going to lose her crown only one month before the end of her reign. I remember, above all other things that day, her attitude. Some of the joy and enthusiasm that had been hers the

last time we met was gone, but not all of it. She told me that morning that she was not going to let this defeat her or take away her dreams. She was going to keep going forward. She wasn't feeling bewildered or sad; she was determined. No matter how far down she would go after that day's appearance, she knew she had the strength and courage to endure it and rise above it.

Vanessa Williams may have been much younger than I was, but she had a lot to teach me. I too was down. I had been in the business for a long time, but it didn't seem like I was going anywhere. I was standing still and had lost sight of some of the goals and dreams I had set for myself. If this fallen Miss America would not be stopped by scandal or misfortune, certainly I could find the strength and motivation to revive my own dreams. Our meeting that day changed the way I looked at my own future; it filled my view of the days ahead with optimism and hope. And it made me see that Vanessa's future would be bright too, despite what was happening on that day. She wasn't in tears; she wasn't blaming others. Vanessa Williams was not going out in disgrace. She was going out as a model of determination in the face of public ridicule and exploitation.

I worked with Vanessa several times after that day. We did a few magazine covers, MTV shows, and performances. I remember once when I was working for *The Oprah Winfrey Show* I saw Vanessa again after a long separation. She was married at that point to her former manager, Ramon Hervey, and she had two beautiful children, Melanie and Jillian, whom I met backstage. I felt so proud of her. She stood there as a mature wife and mother and successful entertainer. She had become the person she had dreamed of all those years ago. Since we'd last spoken, Vanessa had used her spectacular style and relentless drive to reach many of the goals she had told me about years earlier. She had three hit albums, she was a seven-time Grammy nominee, she had twice received the Image Award from the NAACP for her music, and she had starred in a string of television movies. She was only one goal short of having it all.

Knowing this, I can't tell you how excited I felt the night I sat in the audience and watched the curtain rise on Vanessa Williams starring in the Broadway smash hit *Kiss of the Spider Woman*. After the show, I hugged her with warm and heartfelt congratulations. I felt so much emotion for this wonderful young girl who had reached past those who tried to keep her down and found the top of the world.

THE GREAT AMERICAN WEDDING CAKE ▪ WHEN CRACK HITS THE NEIGHBORHOOD

JULY 1988 $2.50

LIFE

THE LADY AND THE CHAMP

TELEVISION'S
ROBIN GIVENS
AND BOXING'S
MIKE TYSON

ROBIN GIVENS

Ambitious, enthusiastic, and sexy are the words that come to mind when I think of Robin Givens. We first met when we did a cover shoot for *Essence* back in 1988. She was different from other celebrities I was used to working with because she was so new to the business—she was naive in some ways, but obviously determined to make her mark. At the time she was doing a TV series called *Head of the Class*, but I knew she had ambitions far beyond the world of sitcoms. *Essence* also knew she was a rising star, and offered her the cover.

Perhaps because she was so young and such a free spirit, Robin was open to new ideas and was willing to try a new look. I thought she had slipped into a stagnant style on TV, and I wanted to use this cover shot to freshen and enliven her beauty. I noticed right away that Robin has a very strong face. Her prominent cheekbones, beautifully set eyes, and full and evenly proportioned lips are well balanced on her face. This was a wonderful canvas to paint—but because it's so inviting, I knew I'd have to resist the temptation to overpaint. That's what happens to a lot of celebrities with perfect features. Makeup artists get carried away, and the women end up looking like painted mannequins. I decided to use a very clean and soft but sexy look on Robin. When I finished, I could see by the look on her face that she loved it. It made a captivating cover that proved my belief that for women like Robin with smooth skin and strong features, less is definitely more.

A month or two later Robin skyrocketed into the eye of the public when she married Mike Tyson, the world heavyweight boxing champion. That's when she called me and asked me to work with her on her appearances—and there were lots of appearances. For the next eight months, we were a team. At one point she and her husband were on the newsstands on five covers simultaneously! We did the covers for *Sports Illustrated*, *Life*, and *People*. Robin was now constantly in demand for magazine stories, TV interviews, commercials, and photo sessions.

Sometimes Robin would want me to drive from New York City to her home in Bernardsville, New Jersey, to do her makeup before an appearance. Many of those times I would do Robin's makeup in her dressing room with the help of Mike Tyson. Not that he would apply any makeup, but because he so much appreciated Robin's beauty, he enjoyed making suggestions that he thought would bring out her best. He might have an opinion on the foundation or blush color, or he would give his preference for lip color. "Let's put her hair up and try red lipstick today," he might say. Often Mike was there to suggest how he would like Robin to look. I always thought this was a very loving and caring attitude.

One of my jobs with Robin really stands out in my memory because it was

truly exceptional from start to finish. Mike Tyson was scheduled to fight Michael Spinks for the world championship at the Atlantic City Convention Center in New Jersey. This would be a big night for Robin too because it would be the first time, as his new wife, that she would be at such a major fight with international media coverage. Of course she wanted to look her best. She sent a Rolls-Royce limousine to pick up me and her hairdresser in New York City and drive us the three hours to Atlantic City. This was typical of Robin; most celebrities don't care how you get to a job—you just get there. Robin made sure we arrived in style. (Her thoughtfulness gave everyone at one McDonald's on the Garden State Parkway a lot to talk about when we pulled up to the drive-in window to order hamburgers. Rolls-Royce or not, we were hungry!)

We arrived in Atlantic City with several hours to spare. This wasn't a job we wanted to rush; we needed plenty of time to do Robin's hair, apply her makeup, and help her pick out the right outfit. When we found out we would also be doing Robin's mother, Ruth Roper, it just added to the fun and challenge of the day.

Robin brought us up to her suite, and we started right in picking out her outfit. After going through her wardrobe, we all agreed she would look great in the red designer dress she had brought with her. Then we spent a lot of time talking about how to make her hair and makeup complement this outfit. It seemed like a good idea to give her a dramatic look, since she would surely catch the camera's eye as she watched the fight. We agreed that her light brown hair would look best in a straight, natural style, and the makeup would have combinations of rust and reds to accentuate her coloring and her dress.

Looking around at what Robin had packed, we realized she needed stockings and earrings. Also, the hairdresser decided he needed a special kind of roller. Off we went to find a jewelry store (not too difficult among the glitz of Atlantic City), a clothing store, and a drugstore (a bit more of a challenge) to

finish her outfit. When we returned, it took several hours to finish both Robin and her mother. I think we were all a bit nervous; it seemed like we were preparing for a premiere—an opening of some kind. In our anxiety to get everything just right, we did and undid our work to perfection. Finally we achieved the look we were going for, and Robin loved it. Although Mike Tyson's day of waiting and preparing was the real story, it felt like Robin was working hard to get ready for her own event.

Ten minutes before the fight started, we left the hotel room and headed downstairs to our reserved seats. As Robin made her grand entrance, we were absolutely floored by the scene in the arena. There were thousands of boxing fans screaming, yelling, stomping, and cheering. The noise and the people were layered so thick in the smoke-laden air that it was a struggle to push our way through to our seats. When we finally made it, we looked around and

ESSENCE

Splash!

Swimsuits That Make Waves

3 Fast Firm-ups

Head Trips to Make You Happy

Body and Soul Food

My 6-Year Battle With Fibroids'

L.A. Law's Blair Underwood

Robin Givens on Beauty, Fitness—and Life With Mike Tyson

Word on Doug Williams, Drug Side Effects, Keith Sweat, Atlanta Sisters

On the Cover:

06

0 14012 34725 1

realized that the fight was over—we had missed the whole ninety-one-second bout that ended with a knockout by Tyson! It had taken three hours to get to New Jersey, four hours to prepare the clothing, hair, and makeup, and ninety-one seconds to miss the whole event. Robin's presence was never noticed until the interviews later that night. I think our biggest mistake was not thinking ahead to explain to Mike Tyson that Robin needed a few minutes to get into the arena and find her seat. If he had known, maybe he could have let the fight go on just a little longer. Only kidding—of course that night was about the fight, and that's what Robin cared about the most.

I last saw Robin on *The Oprah Winfrey Show* a few years ago. Her personal and professional life had gone in new directions, and we hadn't worked together in a while. But I thought she looked great. Keeping with her same free-spirited personality, she had updated her look to move with the '90s. She's young and she's fresh, and she'll never be trapped into one image because she keeps up with makeup and fashion trends.

PATTI LaBELLE

For somebody like me who has been in the business for years, it takes a person like Patti LaBelle to prove that a fab celebrity of renowned talent and prestige can also be just downright nice. Nobody makes you feel more comfortable. Nobody gives you more of herself. Nobody makes you believe more in yourself. And nobody I've met makes you feel more appreciated for the work you do. "Nice" is such a small word, but it describes a very big person. Combine her Grammy-winning five-octave talent with her warm and open personality and you have one of the most special people in showbiz.

I first worked with Patti in 1988 on a black-and-white pictorial that highlighted the accomplishments of outstanding women. Right from the beginning, Patti was welcoming and warm. She was the first celebrity I'd worked with who put *me* up on a pedestal. She knew my reputation and my abilities and didn't hesitate to tell me how happy she was that I had agreed to do her makeup. She made *me* feel like the celebrity.

But before having her own makeup done, Patti explained that her sister, Jacqueline, who was going through a rough time with cancer treatments, was in the studio. She thought it might be fun if I spent some time giving Jacqueline a makeover. This was typical of Patti—she always thinks of others first, and she goes out of her way to make those around her feel good. When I met Jacqueline, I never would have guessed she was ill. She looked wonderful and was as happy and warm as her sister.

Next, it was Patti's turn. Although Patti knew a lot about her makeup, she respected my experience and my talent and gave me the freedom to do what I thought best. This made me feel alive and confident and in charge. Patti is also fun to work with because she likes makeup and she likes the way it makes her feel. When you put a new lipstick on her or you try a new color, she loves it— she gets a kick out of experimenting, and it shows. Following Patti's career, it seems she has had more looks than anyone I can think of. She's gone from that sequined, bouffant, '60s look as the lead singer of Patti LaBelle and the Bluebelles, to the outrageous sparkle and glitter-rock costumes that she wore as the driving force of rock's first all-female band, LaBelle, in the '70s, to the sophisticated look she wears today as a contemporary solo artist.

I think this is part of what makes Patti LaBelle so special—she never stays boxed in one era. Patti always goes out to find change and excitement so she never bores her audience. (Certainly no one was bored during her "Nightbirds" number when, suspended by an invisible wire, she descended to the stage flapping feather-and-fur wings spanning twenty feet!) That's also what's fun about doing her makeup—you never get locked into one look. She's the first to say "go ahead" if I suggest something new or different.

The second time I worked with Patti, she had asked me to do her makeup for a music video she was filming in Minnesota. Some of the video was being shot outside in daylight, so I needed to use a completely different kind of makeup application than we had used on the photo shoot. For outdoor work, you have to be careful not to apply too much makeup that will look harsh or fake under the naked light of day. I couldn't use any strong reds or purples or even fuchsia, which would look heavy in the daylight. For the first time, Patti saw herself wearing a lot of browns with a soft cinnamon tone on the cheeks and a neutral brown on the lips. Instead of contouring the eyelid with color, I used light brown and caramels and just added a dark brown line along the lash line.

For another scene in the video, an indoor scene photographed through a window, I was able to change her makeup, adding more color. I changed the lip color from brown to bronze by adding some tones of coral and brick. I also added more color to her cheeks. Sometimes celebrities (to whom makeup is a routine part of every day) forget that no one particular kind of makeup application is appropriate for every kind of situation, or effective both indoors and outdoors. Patti was a willing student who wanted to learn all about the effects of light on makeup.

There was lots of time to teach her what she wanted to know because video shoots are horribly long—they can run from thirteen to eighteen hours a day. This is not only tough on the performers, it can be very hard on makeup too. In Patti's case, touch-ups were not much of a problem because her skin holds makeup well. Her makeup lasts long because her skin is in such very good condition. All she needed was some moisture to refresh her look, so I spritzed some Evian water on her face.

After the video shoot, Patti, a few friends, and I went out to dinner, where I met another musician I admire greatly—Prince. He had written the music for Patti's video and had spent the day watching the filming. When Patti introduced us, the first thing I noticed was his makeup. (I can't help it—that's always the first thing I look at during an introduction!) I told him that whoever

did his makeup did a fine job. The compliment was returned—Prince told me that he admired the work I had done that day with Patti. He thought she looked terrific.

Since that day when Patti tried the neutral look of browns, I've watched her makeup change to match her music—both are softer and more subtle. She's turned away from the dark and stark contours, from the splashes of purple and pink, and even from her habit of using dark lip liner. When I first met Patti, she used to outline her lips in dark colors to make them stand out. It took her a long time to follow my advice and move away from that. The first time I worked with her, that was the only thing we disagreed on. She had moved into the '80s with her style and music, but couldn't let go of her lip liner. However, after working with me and other makeup artists who also encouraged her to leave it behind, she gradually agreed. (Although I'm sure she snuck it on when those know-it-all makeup artists weren't around!)

I think Patti is now at a point in her career where she's comfortable with herself as a sophisticated, beautiful African-American woman who always looks good from the top of her head to the tip of her toes (especially those shoes!).

THE MAGAZINE FOR TODAY'S BLACK WOMAN

24725 · OCTOBER 1987 $1.50

ESSENCE

Voilà!

Black Paris

- Top Models
- Daring Fashion
- 'In' Spots
- The Beautiful People
- Cooking French

Toni Morrison,
Writing Our World

Wynton Marsalis,
Playing With Fire

Abortion:
Making a Choice

How to Be
Single
and Happy

Word on
Tension Busters,
Yeast Infections, Healing Herbs,
Harlem's Best

NAOMI CAMPBELL

At age seventeen Naomi Campbell came to America from England with eyes wide open in awe, face full of wonder, and great expectations. That was when we first met, and this is the image I'll always carry of this fabulous supermodel. Of course, I had heard about this young sensation because she had made a name for herself on the fashion runways in Europe. But she had not worked in America until *Essence* gave her the opportunity to be on the cover of an issue in 1987 that featured black models in Paris.

Naomi arrived for the magazine shoot carrying her five-foot-nine-and-a-half-inch frame with a grace and sophistication beyond her years. But underneath that outward image was a young girl with fresh, soft skin, a naive spirit, and a youthful eagerness to learn. Having yet to be labeled the "Black Bardot" or the "African Marilyn," Naomi still had an endearing shyness that marked her as a newcomer to this business.

When Naomi came into makeup, she had no idea that she would be leaving with a complete makeover. To gain acceptance in America, she needed a new look; my first job was to convince her that the highly exaggerated, heavily painted makeup used on European runways was not the look she wanted on an American magazine cover. Naomi was obviously surprised to hear about this less-is-more philosophy so popular in America at the time. I think she was hesitant about doing a cover without the heavily painted look she was used to. But I have to say she adjusted quickly. She found that the lighter and softer use of makeup let her own natural beauty become the focus of attention.

It's Naomi's lips that I remember most about this magazine cover—not the shape or balance of them, but the color. I had decided to use a red lipstick for just a bit of drama. We both thought it looked great. But I've noticed that since that cover, Naomi has never been photographed in a full red lip again. After the cover appeared, she must have decided that color wasn't for her. In every photo of Naomi Campbell printed since that day you'll see she wears a soft lip shade.

Fortunately, the red-lip adventure didn't turn Naomi off to my work. After our first meeting, we did several cosmetic print shoots together for big companies like Avon and Revlon. Along the way I made a good friend; this was the first time I became close to a model, and I really enjoyed getting to know this sensitive natural beauty.

One day Naomi called me to her house to prepare her makeup for a New York fashion show. We were in her dressing room talking about the best way to establish a unique look—the thing that makes a model stand out from the crowd. "That's why I call you," she told me. "I've had my makeup done by a lot of people since I've been in New York, but you do the best work when I want

to look natural and soft—that's the makeup that lets me look most like myself." That's the point I was trying to make when Naomi first came to America. It didn't take her long to see for herself that she looks prettiest when she uses her own features to draw the eye to her natural beauty. I remember that this was the first night she wore the soft brown lipstick that I think has since become her trademark. (We definitely weren't going to try red again.)

While preparing for this fashion show, I noticed that Naomi obviously pays close attention to what her hairdressers and makeup artists do. She carefully picks up pieces of information and makes them work for her when the professionals aren't around. She knows how to skillfully manage her hair and how to apply her own makeup. That's why even when Naomi is walking down the street to run an errand, she always looks great. This is a woman who knows how to take care of herself.

This personal know-how also extends to her sense of fashion. Naomi is very fashion conscious, and she knows what she's doing. She knows that just because an outfit is from a top designer doesn't mean the total look will automatically fall into place. As Naomi prepared for that fashion show, I watched her choose just the right shoes, stockings, jewelry, and accessories in a quick five minutes.

Later that evening after the show, Naomi called, and when I answered the phone, I assumed she needed me to do her makeup for a special outing or job. But I was wrong. Instead, she asked me to be her date! Naomi explained that she had to go to a wedding in New Jersey and wanted me to come with her. I don't usually jump at wedding invitations, but I wasn't going to let this one pass by. Of course I would go. When the day arrived, I went to her house early to do her makeup (this was the first time I did a model's makeup and then escorted her out afterward!). Then we drove in my car to New Jersey. I don't have to describe how great I felt; it's not everybody who gets to go on a date with Naomi Campbell.

After the wedding we returned to New York. Thinking my magical date was over, I got ready to take Naomi home. But as we came closer to her house, Naomi surprised me once more by insisting that she buy me dinner at a fabulous Italian restaurant on Madison Avenue.

Shortly after this excursion I left New York to work with Oprah in Chicago. Being so busy, I wasn't able to keep in touch with Naomi over distance and time. But no matter how far apart we are or how many years pass, my date with this wonderful woman is one I'll always remember.

ANITA BAKER

Back in the '80s I fell in love with Anita Baker's rich, deep voice before I even knew her name. I heard her song "Angel" on the radio and was amazed how this voice sounded like an instrument; it was a blending of harmonic tones that I had never heard before. Each time "Angel" would play, I'd rush to the radio to turn up the volume and listen. I wanted to know: Who is this woman? Why don't they ever say her name or the name of the song? I called the radio station to ask but they weren't in the mood to be helpful. I went to a record store to investigate, but no one there was familiar with the song I was humming. Eventually, the single became a hit and the radio announcers were advertising the album and her name: It was *Songstress* by Anita Baker. I bought the album, and I have to admit, I was surprised. This beautiful woman looked too thin and small to be the person who sang those loud, harmonic tones I was intrigued by.

About a year later, we met in person. Anita was chosen for an *Essence* magazine cover photo shoot and I was hired to do her makeup. Anita entered the room a bit shyly, but she greeted us all with a wide smile and a meek apology for being a little late. I could tell right away that this was a nice, down-to-earth person. But I still couldn't believe this small-framed, soft-spoken person had within her the orchestral voice that had stolen my heart.

At this meeting, I think Anita was overwhelmed by the opportunity to do a cover for a national magazine. She was in awe of what went into making it work. All the clothes! All the makeup! All the jewelry! All the people! A fashion stylist, a hair stylist, a makeup artist! It was fun to watch Anita get so excited about all the attention she was receiving.

I had prepared all the colors, formulas, and tools I might possibly need. Anita looked at this spread of equipment and gasped. "You're not going to use all that on me, are you?" She laughed. I explained that I wouldn't use it all at once, but on a job like this I had to be prepared. I never knew what I'd need until I met the celebrity and found out what kind of skin she had, what look she wanted, and what wardrobe and hair style she chose. This was all new to Anita, but she loved it.

When Anita began to prepare for the shoot, she quickly realized that these photos would not portray the same Anita Baker she was used to. The editors explained that they had a certain look in mind and they encouraged Anita to give it a try. The hair stylist, Jeffrey Woodley, cut Anita's hair very short—it was outstanding! The fashion stylist gave her a sexy wardrobe with shapely, off-shoulder styles. We all loved Anita and gave her the attention and support she needed to feel comfortable about her new image.

Anita told me right away that she used very little makeup. She explained how she applied her makeup to create a certain look. She liked a very definite type of foundation, blush, and eye color. She had never considered other possibilities—I convinced her it was time for a change.

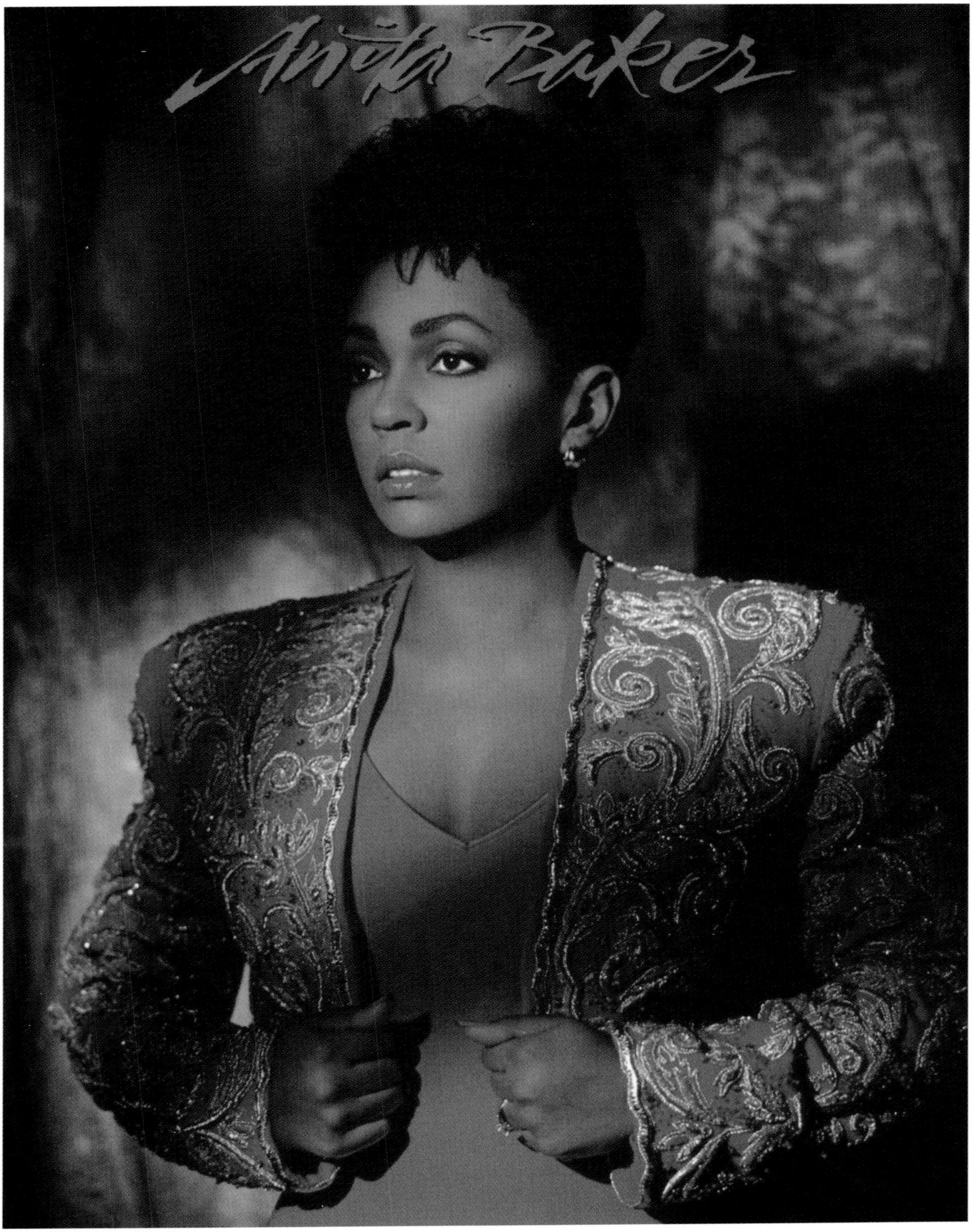
Anita Baker

THE MAGAZINE FOR TODAY'S BLACK WOMAN

34725 DECEMBER 1987 $1.50

ESSENCE

Anita!

She Brings Us Joy

Don't Blame Black Women— A Must-Read

A Story of Triumph You'll Never Forget

Holidays Make You Crazy? Here's Help

Katherine Dunham:
A Living Legend

Challenging Racist Theology

Word on
Festive Fashion, Ski Tripping, Holidays and Single Moms

On the Cover:
ANITA BAKER

12

0 14012 34725 1

Anita has very mysterious and sexy eyes. They are set beautifully in her face. They also have the unique ability to stay wide open even when she smiles. (Most people's eyes squint a bit when they smile.) I told her that we could emphasize the natural beauty of her eyes if we contoured them with one color and lined them with another. Inside the crease I painted magenta and on the rim of her eye I painted purple.

We also talked about using makeup to contour the shape of her face, which Anita felt was too round. I showed her how I could diminish the roundness by drawing a sharp line inside the cheekbone from the earlobe to the cheek area with a medium brown powder blush. Then I blended a wine colored blush on top of this brown to create a soft-looking cheekbone.

Because Anita has such a tantalizing smile, I wanted to highlight her lips. I outlined them with a wine colored pencil and filled them in with a fuchsia gloss. It looked great, and I have noticed that Anita has continued to use this makeup trick herself.

This photo shoot was perfect. Everyone—the fashion stylist, the hair stylist, and myself as the makeup artist—worked together to make Anita feel and look fabulous. Afterward, Anita hired this same group to work with her on her print and TV commercials to advertise the hair product Optimum, by Soft Sheen, for which she became a spokesperson. Obviously, Anita knew what she liked and how to get it. She knew what we were capable of and decided to bring us with her to get the job done right.

Anita continued to introduce me to other opportunities in the business. With her, I gained more experience applying makeup for print advertisements, television, award shows, and videos. She was dynamic and she was everywhere!

Anita is a multitalented person. I loved to watch her do TV commercials because it brought out her dramatic side. She was a perfectionist who wanted every line to be just right. She would go over the wording and phrasing with

the director. She would question the type of delivery they wanted. She was very good. I saw firsthand that Anita not only is an outstanding vocalist, but she is an accomplished actor as well.

Anita is also a gifted musician. She composes many of her own pieces and she plays the piano. Her compositions show that she is a sophisticated woman with deep emotions. When she writes a love song, she has the rare ability to interpret human feelings with the perfect words. I've always believed that the reason she has won seven Grammy Awards is because of this ability. Out of curiosity I once asked her, "What comes first when you write a song—the melody or the lyrics?" "It can happen either way," she confessed. "Sometimes I

hear a melody and later I add the words. Other times I write some lyrics and later add the music."

I especially remember working with Anita in California when she was doing the photo shoot for her *Compositions* album, in 1990. Usually the artist doesn't worry about the creative concept for an album cover, but Anita isn't a "usual" artist. Anita knew exactly what she wanted on this cover. She envisioned a mood that would speak for her music. She saw herself sitting at the piano in deep thought as her fingers rested lightly on the keys. She visualized the placement of the piano by a window with flowers on the side. She knew she would wear a soft and loose sweater.

Anita has grown into a successful, take-charge, artistic woman who knows how to create a visual mood to trigger our emotions. I know it is Anita Baker's artistic talent and vision that keeps her on top.

THE MAGAZINE FOR TODAY'S BLACK WOMAN

34725 · JUNE 1986 $1.50

ESSENCE

SHAPE UP!

The Answers to Your Toughest Questions on Diet, Exercise, Skin and Hair

Work Out With Sports: Five Women Show You How

Saving Our Breasts From Cancer

Eat Well, Stay Fit

● **Luscious, Low-Calorie Foods**

● **The Anticancer Diet**

Swimwear to Suit Your Body

Is It Love or Obsession?

Melvin Van Peebles: How to Win the Money Game

BEVERLY JOHNSON

first saw a photograph of Beverly Johnson when I was in college. I remember thinking that she was absolutely striking. Twenty-some years later, I have the same reaction every time I see her—absolutely striking. Beverly is a legend. In her long and illustrious career as a model, she has graced the covers of more magazines than I can remember—*Cosmopolitan*, *Seventeen*, *Mademoiselle*, *Glamour* (five times in two years!), and *Essence*, to name a few. Of course, most unforgettable was her history-making debut as the first African-American model to appear on the cover of *Vogue*, in August 1974. In 1975, Beverly became the first black model to appear on the cover of *Elle*. Her accomplishments drew worldwide attention to the beauty of black women, and she has held this attention for over two decades.

My first "meeting" with Beverly happened by chance on a street corner in New York. I had just arrived in the city and was trying to get my foot in the door of the fashion industry. I had spent the day showing my book to agencies and had decided to hail a cab and head home. As I reached the curb, I noticed a black woman and two Caucasian women by a telephone booth on the corner. Not trusting my eyes or my luck, I moved a little closer to get a better look. I may have been new to the world of modeling, but I knew who these women were: Beverly Johnson was in the booth talking on the phone and Janice Dickenson and Jerry Hall were waiting for her outside the booth. (Lucky for me, this was the age before the cellular phone!) These women were giants in the industry. I knew their faces like I knew my own. I guess I was staring, but I couldn't help myself. I could see that they were either going to a job or coming from one because although they were wearing casual clothes (designer clothes, I'm sure), their faces were made up professionally. When Beverly finished her phone conversation, the three women stood beside the booth talking. I kept staring. Finally, I got up my nerve and yelled out, "Hi, Beverly." She turned around and my heart began to pound wildly. I waved and she smiled—that's all, just a smile—but it was more than I expected. She didn't know me, of course, but she knew people were bound to recognize her. The next thing I knew, she held up her hand, hailed a cab, and the three of them sped away from the curb. That was the cab I had wanted, but as I stood there with my mouth open, unable to move, they jumped in and were gone. This was my first in-person glimpse of Beverly Johnson. It was quick and it was over before I could gather my wits to say more than hi. But it was a great thrill.

Years later when we worked together, I told Beverly about this moment on a street corner that I will always remember—she had no recollection of it at all, and she couldn't believe I remembered such an inconsequential moment.

My first real meeting with Beverly was years later at *Essence*. We were doing the photos that would accompany an article describing Beverly's skin and health-care routine. This was a unique session for me because the makeup had to look like it wasn't there. The focus was on Beverly's skin itself, not on color or contouring or highlighting. Beverly was perfect for this job. Throughout her years in the business she has managed to escape the aging process. She's managed to keep her facial beauty without being affected by wrinkles. She's managed to keep her body firm. She looks as stunning now as she did in 1971 when she walked into the offices of *Glamour* looking for work. She's incredible. I've never seen anyone who has kept such a youthful appearance.

Doing a job that requires the model to look like she is wearing no makeup was a challenge for me. But with a model like Beverly, it turned out to be easy. Beverly's skin is in the middle tones of brown, so I used just a faint layer of foundation in a soft bronze color. Because she has no uneven skin tones, it was easy to keep the makeup light. One section of the article showed the reader how to use massage creams and lotions, so we needed a shot of Beverly's back. I assumed I would need foundation to even out the different tones that most people have across a large section of skin like the back. But when I placed the massage cream across her back, I found that the skin was exceptionally marvelous. She didn't need any makeup at all—all across her back the skin was smooth and even-toned. It is very rare to see anyone with such naturally beautiful skin, and I knew there was no way makeup could improve on what nature had provided. So this particular shot showed Beverly with no makeup at all—a very daring move for any model except Beverly.

All these years I've carried in my book a shot of Beverly's beautiful face with barely any makeup. It's not the best example of my professional abilities because there was so little to do, but it's the best example I have of the natural beauty of an African-American woman. It's a classic shot of what a woman's skin can be.

After that job I worked with Beverly many more times. We did a piece for *People Weekly*'s February 12, 1990, issue with Christie Brinkley and Cheryl Tiegs. (This setup reminded me of that first glimpse of Beverly when she was with two white women on the street in New York. Except this time she specifically asked for me to be with her!) The shoot was scheduled to introduce Matchbox toys' Real Model doll collection. Beverly, Christie, and Cheryl were each photographed holding the doll with her likeness. My job was to match Beverly's makeup to the makeup on the doll. What a fun day! It was like a reunion for these veteran models who each had made important contributions to the business. They talked and laughed and reminisced. They looked back to marvel at how far they'd come, and they looked forward to where they were going and where they hoped to be in the future.

In between their conversations, the models took a lot of ribbing about their dolls. Certainly it was flattering to have dolls made up in their likeness, but it was also great material for a whole day's worth of good-humored kidding and joking.

Beverly has done a lot more than just break down racial barriers and grab the covers of scores of magazines. She's an intelligent women who is talented in many areas. She has cut two record albums: *Beverly Johnson* and *Don't Lose the Feeling*. She has launched a line of skin-care products. And she has written two books: *Beverly Johnson's Guide to a Life of Beauty* and *True Beauty*. She has also appeared on late-night and daytime television talk shows, served as guest host on Black Entertainment Television, and has acted in everything from music videos to documentaries to Hollywood films to TV series and made-for-TV movies. This woman is not just a model—she's a role model.

The last time I saw Beverly was on *The Oprah Winfrey Show*—it was Oprah's surprise fortieth birthday party. No one working directly with Oprah (or Oprah herself) knew that there would be a wonderful gathering of over-forty celebrities in the audience. My biggest surprise came when I caught sight of Beverly Johnson. As soon as there was a break in the taping, I ran out and threw my arms around her just like I always did in the days of our photo shoots. Without bending the truth an inch, I told her, "You still look as good as ever"—certainly as good as she did in that telephone booth all those years ago.

OPRAH WINFREY

first met Oprah Winfrey on a cover shoot for *Essence* in 1986; I had been hired to do her makeup. As the introductions were made, Oprah jumped back and yelled, "I know you; you're the guy from Baltimore!" It was true— I had first made contact with Oprah years earlier when she began her local TV talk show, *People Are Talking*, in Maryland. At that time I had left my hometown of Baltimore and gone off to do makeup in New York, but on my visits home, I'd see her on television. Over and over I thought to myself that that woman needed me to apply her makeup professionally. Finally, I picked up the phone and called the studio.

Oprah answered her own phone at that time, so it was easy to get in touch, and I told her I wanted to come down to improve her look for TV. "I don't need a makeup artist," she said, and hung up. Over the next month I called constantly because I was convinced that once she gave me a try, she'd like the difference in her appearance. But she was as persistent in saying no as I was in calling her.

Two months later I decided to try a different angle and contacted programming to convince them that I'd make a great guest on the show. They didn't go for the idea. So we never met in Baltimore.

Over the next five years, Oprah and I went separate ways, each of us reaching success in our respective fields. She had been asked to grace the cover of *Essence* because she was nationally known for her talk show in Chicago, and I was brought in because of my reputation as a makeup artist in New York City. Here we were, finally, in the same room. "You're the guy who kept calling me to do my makeup," she laughed. "Yes, I am," I said, "and now you really have to sit still and let me work on you." I guess it was meant to be.

After this meeting Oprah and I worked together for about five years on other magazine shoots and special appearances, including the Oscars. In 1989, I moved to Chicago to become her permanent makeup man for *The Oprah Winfrey Show*.

A CHANGE OF PACE

Taking the job as Oprah's steady makeup artist was a big adjustment for me. I arrived in Chicago just like I had many times before to work with Oprah and other celebrities and companies on a freelance basis. But this time was very different. This was now to be my home—no more commuting back and forth from New York. I was moving in.

Working for a television show was also different from what I was used to—very different. Right in the beginning, Oprah sat me down for a talk. She knew my experience was in covers, magazines, and advertisement shoots, and she knew TV was going to be a challenge for me. Fortunately, she had enough experience with both print and TV to help me through the tough spots. Oprah knew that a major difference would be the timing. I always had anywhere from an hour to an hour and a half to prepare the makeup for a magazine cover, and the environment in a makeup studio was usually calm. But in television time is tight and the atmosphere hectic.

Oprah tried to be patient with me, knowing that everything was so new to me and a bit intimidating. I'd set to work and there'd be a hundred different things going on at the same time. During makeup, phone calls had to be made, questions had to be answered, and producers had to be seen. In the middle of all this, Oprah taught me how to apply foundation and powder in five minutes instead of the fifteen I was used to. Making her eyes up had to be done in ten minutes instead of twenty. To make things even faster, she applied her own false eyelashes, which she did with great speed and expertise. And she showed me how to paint her lips in a flash. (Oprah loves a good lipstick color and was happy with any color I chose—as long as I applied it quickly!)

I soon adjusted to the fast and hectic pace of our makeup sessions, but something was still wrong with the way Oprah's makeup looked on TV. I knew I had to change something, but I wasn't sure what. I studied several old tapes

of the show and I found that the problem wasn't me: The studio lighting was changing the coloring of the makeup along with Oprah's skin tone. Coming from the world of photography, I knew that just the right lighting was necessary to get the most appealing look from makeup, especially on African-American skin. After I pointed out this problem to Oprah, she agreed that it needed to be corrected right away. (Oprah always allowed me complete freedom to do my job and to become involved with the entire process.) I suggested that she have an expert come in to adjust the lighting. This small alteration made a tremendous difference in the appearance of her skin. She looked absolutely fabulous. Small triumphs like this made my time in television worth the stylistic changes and adjustments I'd had to make.

KEEPING UP WITH OPRAH

I was 235 pounds when I went to Chicago. (At five feet six inches I was quite large!) So, at Oprah's suggestion, I joined her and her hairdresser, Andre Walker, on Rosey Daly's diet and began a daily workout in the gym at the studio.

I was trying hard, but one day very soon after I began, Oprah said that she could tell I was lazy and it would be very hard for me to lose weight. That did it—I was out to prove her wrong. (Maybe that was what she had planned.) As a dancer earlier in my life, I had been in great shape and could match anybody's workout routine. Now, at 235 pounds and beginning a month after Oprah, I had to start out more slowly than I wanted (walking before running). The sight of me huffing and puffing on the treadmill started a big joke around the studio that I was going to kill myself trying to keep up with Oprah. There was one day in particular when I thought so too.

It was a spring day and we were on the road out in Iowa; we were taping a show on the book *The Bridges of Madison County*. We were staying in a charming inn on a chicken farm that Oprah loved. But it had no gym facilities like those we were used to in hotels,

and we were scheduled to start shooting the show around 7 A.M. So if we wanted to get in a workout, we had to plan an outdoor run around five o'clock in the morning. I was still new to this running idea but didn't want to admit to Oprah that she was stronger than me. I stumbled out of bed just before five and met Oprah and Andre out front.

The morning sun was barely lighting the running path, and there was a lot of morning dew and fog making it hard to see where we were going through the country lanes and paths that wind around these farms. We set off together, but after just a little while I looked up and found that Andre and Oprah had run off ahead and left me behind. I couldn't see far through the dark and fog, but I knew I was very alone. I didn't know where I was and had lost the trail in the dark. I began running in the opposite direction, thinking I'd meet them back where we started, but I ended up far from the inn on the other side of the road, completely lost. Oprah and Andre thought this was funny and kidded me all day long about my sense of direction and my lack of speed and endurance. I didn't think it was very funny at the time. But I learned something important about Oprah: If you can't keep up, you'll be left in her dust. That was a great incentive to work up to her level.

With the help of Oprah's trainer, Bob, I was soon up to Oprah's pace, running five to eight miles every morning (sometimes twice a day). In the end the effort was worth it for both of us. Over an eight-month period I lost sixty-five pounds and Oprah lost about seventy (managing to beat me again!).

A CREATIVE WORKOUT

Working with Oprah also offered opportunities for creative expression and new experiences. One afternoon, Oprah and I were eating lunch together in the employees' cafe and we were talking art—she was telling me about the artists she admired and her opinions about modern paintings compared to paintings from the Renaissance period. We often had conversations like this because Oprah loved art and she made it a point to have paintings on most of the studio walls. That afternoon I couldn't resist giving my opinion about the two pieces on the cafe wall.

"Who painted these?" I asked.

"I don't remember the artist's name," Oprah said, "but everyone loves them."

"I would guess so, " I replied. "They look like any one of your employees could have painted them! Abstract art seems to be anything that anyone's imagination wants it to be." Oprah laughed. She always respected my artistic opinions even if she didn't agree.

From conversations like this, the Employee Art Program was born— another one of Oprah's ideas to bring her Harpo Productions employees closer together as a family. For three years this phenomenal lady gave me the freedom to offer seminars and workshops in painting, drawing, and sculpting. It was like teaching my school art classes all over again, only this time it was like teaching my family. The employees who signed up loved it and looked forward to each session. Never before had I seen such enthusiasm, not just from the employees but from Oprah herself. She wasn't one of my most talented students, but it never dampened her motivation or spirit. The results were fantastic. People who thought they had no talent at all were beginning to draw and paint fabulous pieces. We were using pencils, oils, watercolors, and acrylics, and sculpting with clay and wood. People who never worked with paint in their lives were amazed. (Some went on to take art classes at the Art Institute in Chicago.) We all met two times a week for eight weeks at a time, and when each seminar was over Oprah celebrated everyone's achievements. She gave the employees the opportunity to display their art work next to the professional paintings in the hallways and in the employees' cafe. The whole experience was very special—it was an activity that brought employees together after work to be creative while sharing their accomplishments and skills.

WORKING ON THE BASICS

My time with Oprah was not all fun and play. During this period I was working on a makeup look for Oprah that would bring out her natural beauty and yet stand up to her long and exhausting days.

Oprah's round face brought her eyes out naturally, but as she lost weight and her cheekbones became more prominent, I needed to emphasize the eyes. I decided to rim her eyes in a lot of dark color. I used eyeliner pencils in strong dark browns and grays. This brought out her eyes for the camera.

Oprah's eyebrows also needed attention—she has very full and wild eye-

ESSENCE ®

MAY 1995
$2.25

25th Anniversary Issue

Wise! Wild! Wonderful!

Oprah Winfrey and 200 Extraordinary Women Who Changed the World

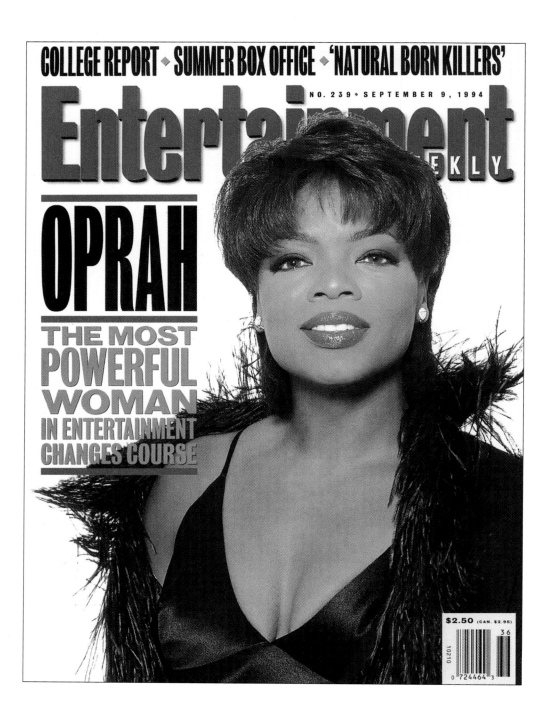

COLLEGE REPORT • SUMMER BOX OFFICE • 'NATURAL BORN KILLERS'

NO. 239 • SEPTEMBER 9, 1994

Entertainment WEEKLY

OPRAH

THE MOST POWERFUL WOMAN IN ENTERTAINMENT CHANGES COURSE

$2.50 (CAN. $2.95)

36

0 724464 3

102210

brows. They need to be shaped, but Oprah can't stand to have her brows tweezed. So I shaved the eyebrows with a standard razor along the bottom rim. I arched the brow and re-created a browline to balance the eye and to give more space to the eye itself. Then I used a dark brown pencil to fill in sparse areas. If you look closely at Oprah, you'll see that her brows are still a strong part of her look, but they don't pull your eye away from her other features and they never look artificial.

Next came the lips. Oprah doesn't have very full lips. Hers are shapely and don't need any reshaping with makeup. They balance out her face because they're not too small or too large.

The base color of Oprah's lips is applied first with a pencil lip stainer painted over the entire lip area. On top of this, the matching lipstick color is applied.

The underlying lip stain is a trick of the trade that keeps the color on the lip and eliminates the need to keep applying fresh color with a lipstick.

Getting this makeup to stay was another matter. Oprah's makeup goes on at about seven every morning and stays on until about seven at night. In the middle of the day, at about two, she needs a touch-up. By this time, a lot of oils will have come through the makeup and become especially noticeable under the camera lights. This is the time to blot the makeup thoroughly with a tissue. (I wouldn't wipe anything off because the makeup has set into the skin by this time and should be left in place.) Then I'd apply a light dusting of a translucent powder over the whole face. The lips need only a moistening with a clear lip gloss. The color from the lip pencil has stained the lips by this time and doesn't wear off even after eating and talking.

I loved working on Oprah's face. She has an inner beauty that shows through her smile and draws the viewer's eye directly to her face.

ESSENCE

JUNE 1991 $2.00

Oprah
Body & Soul

30 WAYS TO BEAT HARD TIMES
FASHION FINDS, $25 TO $100
DINNERS FOR A DOLLAR
FREE ADVENTURES IN BED

THE NEW HAITI
ALICE WALKER'S LATEST

TOUCHED BY AN ANGEL

They say that dreams really do come true, if you hope and pray and keep the faith that there are no doors that can't be opened—working on *The Oprah Winfrey Show* proved this to me. This opportunity was the highlight of my career and the happiest time of my life. It was also the opening I needed to make a lifelong dream come true. I can remember interviewing for a beauty magazine before I started working with Oprah. The interviewer asked me what the future held for me in the beauty industry. In answering I gave many possibilities, but I remember stating specifically that I was dreaming of the day when I would be recognized by my peers for my talent and my skills. In 1985, I accomplished that goal by winning an Emmy Award for doing the makeup on *The Oprah Winfrey Show*. If our paths hadn't crossed, my life goal might still be just a dream.

In the seven years I worked at Harpo Productions I never missed a single workday because I counted myself blessed to be working with such a talented and gifted person. I believe Oprah has been put on Earth for a divine purpose. Every day she reaches out and shares a genuine love that encourages us to believe that each of us has the power to do something positive in the world. No matter what Oprah chooses to do in the future, she will carry with her the love of the millions of people she has touched.

IMAN

The ultimate dream of any new makeup artist is to work with a supermodel. That's the reason we come to New York—we see these models in the magazines, and we want to be a part of their glamour. My big chance came with a call in 1985 to work on an Avon print shoot with the fabulous Iman. By this time I had established my reputation with celebrities and was certainly qualified for this job—still, I was excited, nervous, and thrilled all at the same time. And worried too—I kept looking through my makeup box to make sure I had all the equipment I needed and all the right colors. I didn't want to make any mistakes with my new client, Avon, or appear unprepared to work with Iman.

As I waited, my thoughts drifted back to the designer fashion show where I first saw Iman in person. When I came to New York, I knew the only way I could get anywhere near a supermodel was to get into a designer fashion show and watch her on the runway. Most of the shows were produced on Fashion Avenue, where they have private showings for buyers and fashion magazine editors. Well, I wasn't either of these, but when my friend who worked in the Chanel showroom mentioned he had an invitation to one of the shows, I jumped at the chance. This was a dream come true—every runway model I'd ever wanted to see would be there. What a take-your-breath-away thrill it was to look down the runway and see Iman! She was everything I imagined she would be.

She was a dark, tall, elegant goddess. She radiated a rare beauty that reminded me of the glow that hugs the darkness of a total eclipse. She placed both hands on her hips and began her walk with total confidence. She moved like an object of art—an El Greco painting come alive. Thinking back to this moment, I felt astonished that now her beautiful face would be under the care of my hands.

My thoughts were interrupted by the art director. He wanted to brief me on the dos and don'ts of working for Avon. The idea of such strict guidelines was brand-new to me in this business. I had always created my makeup looks

from instinct and feeling; I always went to the edge and found my own limits. Now I was being told what colors to use, what effect to create, and what style to go for. I understood that Avon wanted to be honest with the public and use their own products in their ads, but these limitations were making me more nervous than I already was. Not only was I to do one of the great supermodels for the first time, but I had to go out of my box, with the colors and blends I was familiar and comfortable with, and into one completely new to me. I was just wondering if I should tell Iman about these restrictions when she arrived.

Iman flew into the room wearing fabulous clothes, a designer hat, and stylish sunglasses. She cried out to everyone in sight, "Darling! I'm sorry I'm late. They gave me the wrong address!" With her sweet, delicate voice with that unique African accent, Iman immediately put everyone at ease.

After our introductions, Iman jumped into an explicit explanation of what kind of makeup she wears and what she won't wear. (She obviously didn't know about the art director's rules!) Iman had her own foundation and powders in a makeup bag she brought with her. As any good makeup artist would do, I said, "Fine!" Because clear, smooth skin is so important to their careers, models can't risk a breakout or a bad reaction by trying out new brands at every job. I learned from Iman that day that good models know what kind of makeup works best on their skin and they bring it with them. I couldn't argue with that. In the end I worked out a compromise between Iman and Avon that satisfied everyone: Because the advertisement was for the color products, Iman would wear Avon color, but she could use her own foundation and powder.

Actually, the powder she used was mine. It was a new formula that I had discovered worked great for dark-skinned women. Most powders use pink-red undertones to complement Caucasian skin, but the orange-yellow base of this powder matched the natural undertones in black skin. Iman was very curious about the formulas and color tones of makeup. She asked a lot of questions and showed an intellectual interest in cosmetics. She liked this powder so much that after the job, she asked me to come to Bloomingdale's with her so she could buy some for herself—she bought five or six pots!

There was a lot of give and take that day between Iman and me. Iman learned something new about face powder, and I learned why models like to use the makeup that they're accustomed to and that I should expect most good models to have their own. I'm always open to learning new things and welcomed anything Iman could teach me.

I got a good feel for Iman's helpful personality and professionalism during the shoot, but I wasn't prepared for

what happened once the lights went up and the modeling began. Iman doesn't just model; she works the camera with astounding talent. Avon was selling lipstick and eyeshadow, and to do that, Iman assumed the dramatic attitude of an actress talented enough to be nominated for an Academy Award in a major motion picture role. With great dramatic flair, she opened her eyes wide and then shut them slowly as if moving in slow, altered time. She winked demurely. She teased and tanta-

lized the camera. She turned her head quickly and skillfully. She caressed her lips with her fingers and then pulled her arms up over her head. The photographer, amazed by her energy and elegance, paused to catch his breath. The client was obviously pleased and impressed by her charisma. Looking back on this session, I can understand why the term "supermodel" was invented to describe women like Iman. At that time the term "top model" was used for the best in the business, but today she is known around the world as a supermodel.

Iman deserves the title of supermodel, but it is only a part of who she has become. She's still modeling, of course—she has recently had a contract for Donna Karan's line of clothes. But she's gone beyond the expected and into the business world. The astute and savvy businesswoman inside her was obvious, even in '85, from the way she knew the details of her makeup, the way she was so interested in a new product, the way she was conscious of where the cosmetics industry was going, and the way she knew how makeup can affect attitude and self-image—all these things would come together to make her a very successful businesswoman. Today she has her own major cosmetics line, called Iman, formulated specifically for black women. Her years of modeling taught her what works on dark skin and what doesn't.

DIAHANN CARROLL

After being in the business for twenty years, I was recently asked if there was any celebrity that I hadn't worked with yet but really wanted to. Without hesitating, I said, "Yes—Diahann Carroll." I had always admired Ms. Carroll and looked up to her. So it bothered me that I hadn't had the opportunity to do the makeup of one of the most beautiful African-American women in the world. Right then I decided that I should try to arrange to meet her.

I figured the most direct route was through a friend of mine who was Ms. Carroll's hairdresser. I gave him a call and asked if he could *please* put in a good word for me with Diahann. It wasn't long after that that Ms. Carroll asked my friend if he could recommend a makeup artist for an on-camera interview she had scheduled. Sure enough, my friend gave her my name and I got a call!

I hurried to New York for the job. In my rush, I hadn't had time to think, but as I stood outside her apartment building ringing her bell, I was suddenly overcome with doubt. Did I bring the right equipment? Did I pack the right colors for her complexion? How should I do her eyes? Well, ready or not, here I was—but no one was answering. I rang the bell again and waited. Still no one came. With each minute that passed, I grew more nervous. Now I worried: Did I have the right date? Was this the right address? Did anyone tell her I was coming? I rang again. After about ten minutes, a casually dressed woman, holding a book and wearing glasses, opened the door. I was about to ask for Ms. Carroll when I realized it was her! I would never have guessed that the first words this talented and legendary woman would say to me would be "I'm so sorry." She had been reading in the back of the house and didn't hear the bell.

She invited me into her home, and we walked down a long hallway to her great room, where she invited me to make myself comfortable and wait for her return. As I looked around, I saw that I was in an enormous room that was beautifully decorated with fine antique furniture. The elegance of the room mirrored its owner. As more time passed, my nervousness returned. Knowing I was about to work with one of my idols—a Tony Award winner and an Oscar and Emmy nominee—it was difficult just to sit around without working up a nervous sweat. I needed something to take my mind off my fears. Soon I spied a stack of books on the coffee table—they were large, colorful books about music, photography, and art. These grabbed my interest and calmed my jitters while I waited for Ms. Carroll.

About a half hour later Diahann returned, dressed in her robe and ready for makeup. She apologized for the delay and led me to her dressing room. As we entered, I noticed a counter that held an impressive assortment of makeup. Diahann had her own collection of sponges, tweezers, brushes, foundations, blushes, eyeliners, mascara, lipsticks, and so on. When I opened my makeup bag, she suggested that I could probably find everything I needed in her own collection, hinting that these were the things she was most comfortable using. Obviously, I had worried for nothing about having the right makeup with me. Ms. Carroll had enough experience with her makeup and the details of her appearance that I needn't have been so concerned. Ms. Carroll was more than willing to tell me exactly what she wanted.

Under her careful direction, I was very comfortable applying each type of makeup just as she liked it. I should mention that it's very unusual for a celebrity to have such an array of personal makeup and tools. But Ms. Carroll knew what worked best for her, and she knew she could communicate to me exactly what she wanted if she had what I needed close at hand. She told me how to put on her foundation and how to blend it. She also pointed out which powder to use and how to apply it to make it look smooth and natural. She told me the kind of facial contouring she wanted and how to apply the makeup to achieve it. She chose the color she wanted on her face, and she instructed me on how to do her eyes to make them stand out and look strong. She also told me which blush and lipstick to use. This was a woman who knew her own look. For me, it was an exciting day of following instructions and learning new things. I remember that Ms. Carroll taught me about the effect of light from certain angles and how it dictates the placement of her makeup. Her theatrical experience taught her that there are certain unique lighting considerations you have to be aware of when you apply makeup. (At the time she was performing the role of Norma Desmond in *Sunset Boulevard*.) Since my previous work had been with celebrities in print, TV, and concert performances, there was a lot I could learn from this diva of the stage.

Once Ms. Carroll took charge, my nervous jitters eased and a comfortable conversation began. Right away I told her why I admired her and how I came to be her number one fan. It happened in about 1970 when I was in my basement watching television on a Saturday around eight o'clock. The variety show *The Hollywood Palace,* which featured singers and dancers, came on, and Diahann Carroll was the guest star. I remember her coming out onstage in a white gown with her hair swept up beautifully in the style of the time; she sang the Beatles tune "Here, There, and Everywhere" with a completely new and unique arrangement. At that moment, I became a lifelong fan. She not only gave a new style to this well-known tune, but she gave her audience a piece of herself with emotion and drama.

"I still remember the arrangement of that song," I told her.

"How could you?" she challenged me. "It was so long ago."

"It's easy to remember everything about the moment I fell in love with you as a performer, a singer, and a lady," I told her as I began singing the song with her arrangement. Then I heard her wonderous voice take over the next line.

We both burst out laughing.

"You *do* remember!" she marveled.

I told Ms. Carroll that after that show I went out and bought every album she had ever recorded. In a specialty store I even found the original cast recording of the Broadway play *No Strings* in which she starred in the '50s and for which she won a Tony Award.

We passed the time in that makeup session singing songs from her albums that many others have forgotten. It was great fun. I not only knew all the words, but I could also imitate Ms. Carroll's gestures as I sang.

"When you get going," she laughed, "you look just like me!"

"That's because I'm such an admiring fan," I reminded her.

I have great respect for Ms. Carroll. To me, she is the epitome of a great lady. I know this is a bold statement, but it's true. Diahann Carroll is an intelligent, talented, glamorous, good, and charismatic person. And I owe more to her than simply the joy I've experienced from following her career. Seeing

Diahann on *The Hollywood Palace* so many years ago did more than open my eyes to this great performer; it also inspired me to get into the business. Her appearance on television that night back in 1970 reminded me that African-American women are endowed with natural style and glamour, and that I needed and wanted to be a part of this emergence of their true beauty.

ARETHA FRANKLIN

W hen you hear the phrase "Queen of Soul," you might think it's a label made up by some PR department to sell a celebrity image. But when we're talking about Aretha Franklin, "Queen of Soul" is no hype. It's a title that has been bestowed with respect and sincerity by the media, fellow musicians, and fans alike. Aretha is an established giant in the industry who possesses a natural sense of dignity and talent, and I've always felt honored to work with her.

I first worked with Aretha in 1986 in Detroit, her hometown. Since then I have done her makeup for many appearances—from Caesar's Palace, to commercial and video shoots, to album cover shoots, to Carnegie Hall, to President Clinton's birthday party, to the 1996 Democratic convention and the 1997 Inaugural Ball. On all of these occasions, I've noticed that others always defer to this beloved performer. Everyone, the stage crew, the director, the photographer, the conductor—no matter how famous or renowned—is aware that they are working with a queen, and they willingly show her much respect.

I remember this feeling was especially strong during one particular party. Aretha flew me into Detroit to do her makeup before a high tea she was having in her home. This was the first time I had been to Aretha's house, and I was immediately taken with its sophisticated atmosphere. When I walked in the door, I knew this was the home of a musical legend. My eyes were drawn to side walls, which were decorated with her fifteen Grammys and her 1990 Lifetime Achievement Grammy. Another wall displayed photographs showing Aretha with President Bill Clinton and industry giants like Lena Horne and Sam Cooke. In a world where singing stars come and go, Aretha reigns supreme with her distinctive soulful sound—beginning with her debut single and million-seller, "I Never Loved a Man," thirty years ago in 1967, and continuing through her latest million-seller, *Aretha Franklin Greatest Hits*. No wonder the Michigan legislators have proclaimed her voice to be one of the state's natural resources!

I could have spent the day admiring her many accomplishments, but I had work to do. After twenty years in the business, you'd think I could just walk in and do her makeup easily—but I knew better. Aretha always has something new to tell me about the way she wants her makeup applied, and I always need to leave a little extra time to listen and follow her instructions.

I learned quickly that you don't go to Aretha with new or preconceived ideas. This is a woman who has a very clear picture of exactly what she wants and the best way to get it. The way she pays particular attention to the shape of her eyebrows is a good example of how carefully she directs her makeup application. She tells me exactly where and how to draw her brows. It's not

just any brow—it's her unique brow with an arch that's drawn under her careful instruction. Sometimes she makes me nervous because it's not always easy to make the brow look exactly as she imagines it should. But I keep trying; she knows how high the arch should go, where it should come back down over her eye, and how dark it should be colored. I just have to keep at it until it's right. Aretha will also tell me what lipstick color she wants. She'll choose the foundation and the coloring for her face. She has an artistic eye for what's best for her in each situation. If she's after a particular stage look, she'll tell me how she wants to appear, knowing I can give it to her. When she wants a certain look for a video, she can describe it to me and feel confident she'll get it. There are no surprises for Aretha—I think I've learned over the years how to accommodate her.

After our midafternoon makeup session, Aretha insisted that I join the party. What a great opportunity for me! I could see immediately that the atmosphere fit Aretha Franklin's queenly image. All the guests (who included every society figure in the city and beyond, from the mayor to the governor, from celebrities to professors) were elegantly dressed and looked quite refined. Aretha too was dressed beautifully in an afternoon suit and a matching hat with a short veil. In the background a large group of musicians played a mixture of jazz, R&B, and classical music. Caterers elegantly served an array of finger sandwiches, appetizers, meats, vegetables, petits fours, and pastries in buffet

style and, of course, tea or coffee. What a wonderful way to get to know Aretha, not only as a musical great but also as a warm and gracious person.

Aside from her personal charm and hospitality, Aretha Franklin will be forever admired in the industry as an incomparable professional. I am convinced of this, especially after watching her performance at the Kennedy Center for the Performing Arts' celebration of the Public Broadcasting System (PBS). People from different areas of the arts, from dancers to poets, from pop singers to operatic divas, from actors to composers, were all invited to Washington, D.C. for this celebration. I remember watching Aretha make her stage entrance in an absolutely beautiful long, mist green gown with a three-foot train as she went out to sing the finale for the program. As her song ended, she stood in the front bowing to a standing ovation while all the other performers stood behind her for their own bows. This is how I will always picture Aretha Franklin—out in front, given respect by all others. This is truly the Queen of Soul.

CHAKA KHAN

Chaka Khan was full of laughter the day we worked on her 1996 *Essence* cover. She was having a great time, and her vibrant personality just bounced off the walls around us. I have to admit: I was shocked. I didn't expect this kind of fun and easy atmosphere when I was hired to work with this great entertainer. That day the woman I met was not the same Chaka I had met years earlier.

In 1986, I was hired to do Chaka's makeup for a TV interview. When she entered the room, she let me know right away that she didn't need anybody to do her makeup. Of course, this surprised me. Most of my celebrity clients knew my reputation as an artist and were glad to have me on the job. Not Chaka— she wanted nothing to do with me. Finally, she reluctantly let me put some powder on her face, but she certainly didn't pretend to like it. I didn't take all this personally. I figured that Chaka was the kind of lady who liked to control everything about the way she looked, and she was not into having people fuss over her. So I just gave her some powder, left, and didn't expect to see her again. And I didn't—until our meeting at *Essence* almost ten years later.

When I told Chaka about our last meeting, she laughed. She didn't remember the incident, but she apologized with the confession that it must have been one of her really bad days. But now we had a chance to start over, and I'm so very glad we did because as it turns out, there are very few people in the business with whom I now feel so comfortable working.

If you know Chaka, you know that she likes to wear makeup. But for this cover shoot, she was willing to let me try something new. I wanted to make her look softer and fresher than usual. First I changed the way she darkens her eyes with dramatically deep-colored eyeshadow: I used a light, neutral tone to make her eyes look more open. I did the same on her lips; instead of her usual dark colors, I applied a soft fuchsia and let some of her natural color come through. I made the cheekbones soft instead of contouring them to make the bones stand out. While making these changes, I had to remember that Chaka doesn't want to copy anyone else—she is uniquely Chaka. Even though her new look for this magazine cover was different, it still had to be something fresh and unrivaled—something that still flattered and accented the "Chaka" look. The result was soft and at the same time bold—and she loved it!

Unlike the first time we met, after this job I knew I would hear from Chaka again. Almost immediately we did several more photo shoots and then ventured into a job that was like no other I'd ever had before. Chaka asked me to go with her on a promotional tour for her album *Epiphany,* which was released to celebrate her twenty-fifth anniversary in music. This trip brought us together for nine days and gave me the opportunity to get to know the beautiful, vivacious, and full-of-fun woman that she really is.

CELEBRATING OUR **25**TH ANNIVERSARY YEAR

OCTOBER
1995
$2.25

ESSENCE

CHAKA
The Wild Child Finds Peace

Secure Your Financial Future Today!

Single Mothers' Survival Guide

Race in Your Face
Black and White America Talk About Each Other

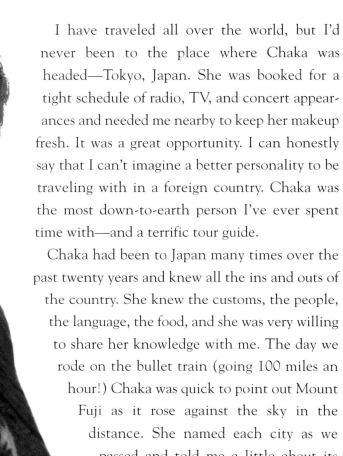

I have traveled all over the world, but I'd never been to the place where Chaka was headed—Tokyo, Japan. She was booked for a tight schedule of radio, TV, and concert appearances and needed me nearby to keep her makeup fresh. It was a great opportunity. I can honestly say that I can't imagine a better personality to be traveling with in a foreign country. Chaka was the most down-to-earth person I've ever spent time with—and a terrific tour guide.

Chaka had been to Japan many times over the past twenty years and knew all the ins and outs of the country. She knew the customs, the people, the language, the food, and she was very willing to share her knowledge with me. The day we rode on the bullet train (going 100 miles an hour!) Chaka was quick to point out Mount Fuji as it rose against the sky in the distance. She named each city as we passed and told me a little about its people, industry, and history. This wasn't work; it was like a marvelous vacation.

On another day Chaka took me to an open food market, where we went from vendor to vendor trying new things. The sights and sounds and smells were all so exotic to me but second nature to Chaka. Then we stopped at a very traditional Japanese restaurant to experience the customary way of dining. That day alone I ate sushi and grilled eel, and I drank sake. I would never have tried these things (or figured out how to use the yen to pay for them!) if I had been traveling alone. Chaka was my guide and support. We really enjoyed our nine days—and still found time to get the job done.

One afternoon was especially busy. We went to a radio station for an on-air interview and then to a record store for an autograph signing. I watched in amazement as the crowds lined up to meet Chaka and she spoke in Japanese as best she could. We left the store in a great mood. During the ride back to the hotel, I put on her new CD and absentmindedly started singing a few bars of

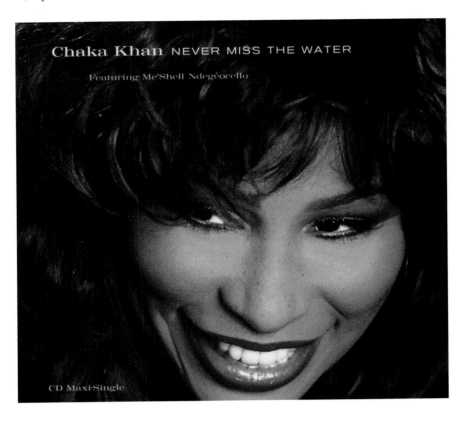

my favorite song, "At the End of a Love Affair." The next thing I knew, Chaka was singing right along with me. We were belting out a duet—me with my flat, low baritone voice trying to keep up with her trained alto voice. How many professional singers can stand by and listen to their song being butchered by an off-key amateur? Chaka can. She just sang along with me wearing that smile that takes over her whole face. When the song ended, Chaka searched hard for something to say that would sound like a compliment and finally offered, "You sure do know all the words."

The whole tour was a professional and personal experience I'll never forget. Hopefully I'll be spending even more time with Chaka in the future—at this point, we've already committed to doing some music videos together. I think we work well together because Chaka knows I would never try to change her unique style—I work along with it to keep her fresh and always new.

I just hope I can keep up with her energy level. With homes in Germany, England, and Los Angeles, Chaka jets around like a super lady, always on the run. But wherever she is, she is sure to have family around her. Chaka's mother is her finance manager; her sister Tammy is her manager; and Tammy's husband, Howard McCrary, is her musical director. Chaka's brother, Mark, sometimes tours with her as a backup singer, and her son, Damien, her daughter, Milini, and her granddaughter, Raeven, are often by her side.

I had a lot of fun with Raeven at a concert of Chaka's in Chicago. Raeven was going to perform a song onstage with Chaka, so she wanted me to do her makeup. I sat her down and fussed over her, gave her the makeup she'd need under the lights, and sent her out to sing with her nana. Those two are a great pair; Chaka just glows when Raeven is around. Chaka once told *Jet* magazine, "Some people are ashamed to say, 'I'm a grandmother or a grandfather now.' But I have no problem with that because I absolutely love being a grandmother. [Raeven] is the sweetest thing to happen to me in seventeen years."

This ability to love so strongly is a part of Chaka's appeal to her fans too. In any country she is at home and her fans love her. They give her love and she gives it right back to them. For all these reasons, I have no doubt that Chaka Khan will be an outstanding entertainer for at least twenty-five more years. And it's my hope that I will still be the one powdering her face while singing her music off-key.

SUSAN L. TAYLOR

Back in the '70s I was an avid reader of *Essence*—a magazine that right from the start stood out from the others. *Glamour*, *Vogue*, *Seventeen*, and the rest ignored the strength of ethnic pride in African-American women. They knew nothing about the black woman's fashion, styles, or color. Only *Essence* celebrated this heritage and beauty. I remember checking the masthead for the name of the fashion and beauty editor who had such a creative and strong hand in molding the slant of the magazine. It was Susan L. Taylor. It was clear that she was interested in black women in their entirety. That was how I first became acquainted with the name and work of this talented and inspirational woman who later was to have a profound effect on my career.

It wasn't until ten years later that I had the chance to see Ms. Taylor in person. I had moved to New York to begin my career and had the opportunity to attend a function at which Susan was the guest speaker. She stood up front looking proud and polished like one of the models she presented on the pages of her magazine. She was tall and regal; her clothing, hair, nails, and makeup were all impeccably done. But her beautiful appearance was only the wrapping around her real inner beauty. As soon as she started to speak, I knew this was a very reflective and sincere person. Her message was not about the latest styles, as you might expect from a fashion editor. Instead she spoke from the heart about following dreams and making it in life. She stood before this audience as an example of determination as she talked about her own experiences as a single mother from Harlem who worked hard to turn her life around, keep her family together, and succeed at her very demanding job. She reminded us that she had been with *Essence* when it was just starting out in an East Side brownstone. She was there when the magazine first began drawing national attention for its unique focus on African-American women. She was there when everyone worked through the night to make it happen. Susan Taylor not only knew how to dream, she knew how to make dreams happen.

This kind of motivational talk was just what I needed at that time. I had come to New York with big dreams but was having trouble making them come true. I was feeling very low and was on the verge of giving up. Then I heard her words; it was as if she were talking directly to me and encouraging me to keep at it. She made me believe that I could make it in New York—this place where rejection was the norm, where survival was never guaranteed, and where dark days were constant companions. I left that room with the drive I needed to endure the tough days (while selling makeup in department stores) and keep my eye on the prize ahead—becoming a successful makeup artist. That day Susan Taylor gave me my start in the business. Long before she and I met personally and she hired me to work with cover models for *Essence*, Susan gave me what I needed to be successful—belief in myself.

After this meeting, things didn't suddenly get easier for me. There were still many depressing days, but I had Susan's words to keep me going. Again and again I would hear her words about reaching for dreams and making them happen, and I would be back at work giving it my all.

As I began to get occasional freelance makeup jobs, I was able to put together a good portfolio of my work. I was proud of these photographs showing beautiful women wearing my makeup applications. I was ready to take this book to agencies and magazines and pave my way to success. The first person I thought of was Susan Taylor. I knew I'd love to work for *Essence*, and since she herself had given me the motivation to make it this far, it made sense that I should go to her to complete the last step toward realizing my dream.

As we began our interview, I reminded Susan of her presentation years earlier and thanked her for her motivational words. She smiled and nodded without looking up from my book. This was nerve-racking; her face gave me no clue about her thoughts concerning my work. Fortunately, I didn't have to sweat it out for very long. In her trademark straightforward and up-front style,

Susan told me that I wasn't ready for *Essence*. She liked my work and found it creative, but she knew that makeup application for Caucasian women is very different than it is for black women. "I can't judge your work from this," she said. "You need to get more experience with black women." I didn't think there was any difference in applying makeup to Caucasian women or black women. Makeup was makeup. It just so happened that the models I had gotten the opportunity to work with were white.

About eight months later I went back to *Essence* with my new portfolio full of African-American women. Now Susan was impressed. She booked me on the spot for an upcoming beauty story. This was the sign of approval I had been working for; with a simple nod of the head, Susan made my dream come true. But before she turned me loose on the set, Susan and another beauty editor, Sandra Martin, sat me down to explain how they wanted the makeup to be applied. They told me the colors they thought looked best on black women; they showed me the foundation that gave the best coverage and appearance. Before becoming an editor and a journalist, Susan had been a cosmetologist who owned her own cosmetics company with products marketed to African-American women. She knew what she was talking about. She was continuing my education and helping me learn how to skillfully apply makeup for print photography. She was a terrific teacher.

After this introductory lesson, I did a lot of work with *Essence*. Susan opened this door for me. She gave me skills, knowledge, drive, and, in the end, the work that allowed me to build my reputation.

In addition to working for *Essence*, I've also had the honor of doing Susan Taylor's makeup for the last seven years. She selects me to do her makeup before photo sessions and appearances because she knows I understand exactly what she wants to look like. I don't do her face the way I would do anyone else's—her look is unique. She has beautiful, youthful skin that can handle the less-is-more makeup look. Her almond-shaped eyes are a strong feature that I

accentuate by using a thin liner around the eye and extending it out onto the eyelid. I use an even foundation application because Susan's face is so finely structured that it doesn't require any contouring or highlighting. I finish with a strong lipstick in berry or wine tones to complement her medium brown skin and to draw attention to the wonderful shape of her lips. She is comfortable with this look, and although we've added some changes over the years, with a perfect canvas like Susan's it's always best to stick to the basics.

Of all the wonderful, beautiful women I have worked with, it is Susan Taylor who has stayed with me through every step of my career. From our first meeting in 1983 when I was looking for work to today when I do her makeup before important appearances, this woman has been my inspiration. It is to Susan Taylor that I owe the greatest debt of gratitude. Her guidance, her teaching, her motivation, and her faith in my talent have combined to allow me to reach my dream of drawing media attention to the natural beauty of African-American women.

SPECIAL COLLEAGUES

Jeffrey has been a leading hair stylist for over a decade and has worked with a number of celebrities including Diahann Carroll, Jody Watley, Angela Bassett, and Faith Evans. He has greatly influenced my life and my career because we have worked together on a number of commercials, videos, and the cover shoots for *Essence* magazine—without his expertise in styling I'm sure I would not have made some of the makeup choices that have brought my work attention and praise. Although Jeffrey has made a commitment to the entertainment industry that has been recognized nationally, he still works in his salon in New York City with his regular customers. Here his clients are treated like

celebrities by this charming and elegant stylist, and they all get more than just a hair style—they get an education. Being highly trained himself, at the Sasson School of Hair Design, Jeffrey wants his clients to feel like they've learned something when they go home; he wants them to know how to manage their hair, how to treat it, how to maintain the style. The theory behind the style is as important to this talented man as the style itself. He is a major force in the industry and in my life.

ANDRE WALKER: THE MAN BEHIND THE STYLE

I first met Andre Walker when I went to work for Oprah Winfrey. He immediately struck me as a gentle, yet sophisticated giant, and thankfully, he was gracious enough to help me adjust to the world of television. I came to *The Oprah Winfrey Show* with a background in print work, and it was Andre who shared with me his expertise in the effects of lighting, movement, and live filming on the total look of television entertainers. When we would start a new season with Oprah, we would want to give her a new look. Without Andre's knowledge and vision, I think it would have been very hard for me to come up with new makeup ideas each year. But with Andre's guidance and creative styling ideas, it worked every time. It is no surprise to me that he has won six Emmy Awards. (In fact, I feel I owe my own Emmy nominations and award to the partnership we created during those years in television.) Even now when I see his work, I'm always impressed by the strength of his style. Andre deserves the credit he has earned as one of the most respected, artistic people behind the scenes in the television industry today.

PART III

BEAUTY
SECRETS

MAKING THE EYES THE FOCAL POINT OF THE FACE

Not only does she have the world's brightest smile, but Whitney Houston also has eyes that shine like the star she is. Her dark eyes are beautifully balanced in shape and size, giving her the most wonderful eyes in the business. I have a special attraction to eyes because I believe that the eyes of an African-American woman reflect her soul; painting the eye brings out the depth and beauty of this deep, inner spirit.

To bring out the best in your eyes with makeup, you have to know what kind of eyes you have. Are they normal, large, deep-set, small, or droopy? Each type of eye requires a different approach to makeup application, so each is explained separately in this chapter.

To get the perfect effect from eye makeup, you also have to consider your skin tone. There are many shades of dark skin—and each one requires a different color eye makeup. (You'll learn more about this in the makeover lessons in Part IV, where you'll find color charts to help match your skin tone to your makeup colors.) For women with medium brown skin, I like to use the full range of browns (all the monochromatic colors from light beige to dark brown). On women with very dark brown skin, I use the full spectrum of purples (all the monochromatic colors from light fuchsia to deep purple). And on women with light brown skin, I use the different shades of coral (all the monochromatic colors from light peach to rust). I've found that these colors accentuate the natural beauty of the eye and pull the focus away from any flaws.

After applying the liner and shadow as explained below, I use black mascara, usually on the upper lashes only. Most problem features appear under the eye, and mascara on the bottom lashes will draw attention to them—dark circles, bags, uneven skin colors, and wrinkled skin become more obvious if the bottom lashes stand out.

NORMAL EYES

Normal eyes have no obvious flaws or problems that need to be camouflaged with makeup.

If you have normal eyes, you're one of the lucky ones and should use eye makeup sparingly. Let the natural beauty of your eyes speak for itself.

Use a light application of shadow, liner, and mascara. On light brown skin, you would select a shadow in the coral tones that complements your skin color. Apply the shadow evenly from the lash to the eyebrow.

Use a liquid liner in brown or black. Draw a thin and even line close to the lashes on the top lid. Don't put any liner by the lower lashes.

Apply one coat of mascara and you're done.

LARGE EYES

Eyes that are large and open draw immediate attention to the eye area.

If you have large eyes, you want to hold a person's attention on your eyes. However, you don't want to use loud or bright colors that would overemphasize the fullness of your eyes. You don't want your eyes to be the only thing that shapes the beauty of your face.

You can enhance the impact of large eyes by circling them with natural colors that complement your skin tone. Choose an eye shadow color that's just slightly darker than your natural skin color. If you have medium brown skin, for example, you would choose a medium brown shadow to circle around your eye. It doesn't matter what *type* of shadow (powder, stick, etc.) you use—it's the color that counts. As if it were an eyeliner, run the eye shadow all around the eye on the upper lid and below on the lower rim close to the lashes.

Then, with an eye pencil, lightly paint inside the bottom rim with a color that's on the dark end of your color spectrum. With medium brown skin, you would use a dark brown or black pencil. This will make the eye appear just slightly smaller.

Next, paint the skin from the eyelid crease to the brow with a color that's just a bit lighter than your natural skin tone. On medium brown skin, you might use beige or caramel.

These techniques will highlight the beauty of your large

eyes, while reducing their tendency to absorb too much of the focus on the face.

DEEP-SET EYES

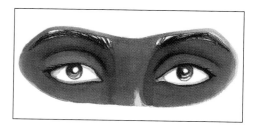

Deep-set eyes have a pronounced crease with a very visible lid.

If you have this kind of eyes, you're very lucky. The drama and character of deep-set eyes is already there—you have the most naturally perfect type. Your eyes have their own mysterious quality even without makeup, so there's no need to use dramatic makeup applications to over-emphasize any aspect of the eyes. Less is best.

Deep-set eyes require that you use color sparingly, so paint them with only the slightest bit of makeup. The shape of the deep-set eye makes its own shadow naturally because of the perfect placement of the crease in the lid. If you have deep-set eyes, never place dark shadow in this crease. Paint only the lids of your eyes. You don't need to add any more darkness in the crease area.

On deep-set eyes you should use eye shadow colors that are on the light end

of your color spectrum. If you have very dark brown skin, you can use light fuchsia on the lid (staying away from the crease).

Then rim your eyes (above and below) with a shadow that is slightly darker than the shade you used on your lid. If you have very dark skin and you used fuchsia on the lid, you could use a wine color to rim the eyes.

Next, paint the area just under the eyebrow (staying away from the crease in the eyelid) with the same color you put on your lid.

Too much makeup detracts from the natural beauty of deep-set eyes—it ruins something that is already lovely. Using the natural colors that complement your skin tone will add beauty to your eyes without putting unnecessary emphasis on them.

SMALL EYES

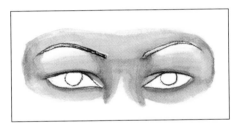

Small eyes are those that are proportionately smaller than your other facial features. They need makeup that will make them look wider and more in balance with the rest of your face.

If you have small eyes, you can use a lot of color in your eye shadow, but never put dark liner on the inside lower rim; this will make the eye look even smaller! To widen the eye, use colors in your color spectrum that are just a bit lighter than your natural skin color. Never use colors that are darker than your skin tone; they also make the eyes look smaller. If you have light brown skin, you might use a peach color.

Paint your eye shadow color in an upward and outward motion from the inner corner of your eyelid through the crease at the center of the eye; then extend it out to the end of the eyebrow. The skin under your brow in the area closest to the nose should not be colored. Moving the color from the inner corner of the eye to the outmost end of the brow will enlarge the appearance of the eye.

Rim below your eye with this same color and paint it in an upward motion to meet the eyelid color at the end of the brow. Because the end of the eyebrow goes beyond the end of the eye, moving the makeup in this direction extends and elongates the eye.

Close to the lashes of the upper and lower eye, add an eye shadow color (as you would an eyeliner) that's a shade darker than you used on the lid. On lighter skin with peach shadow, use a light rust. But don't rim all around the eye. Start at the area above and below the center of the pupil and draw it out

to the end of the eye. Extend this color from the lid of the eye in an upward motion to blend in with the lighter shadow on the lid.

To open up the eye even more, you might want to try this little trick: Use a white eye pencil to color the inner rim of the lower lid.

THE DROOPY EYE

This eye has lost the elasticity in the skin below the brow. It droops down and covers the eyelid.

It is very important to know how to paint the eye with a droopy lid so it looks its best even when the eye is open and the eyelid disappears. If you put too much effort into painting the lid of this eye, you're wasting your time—no one can see it! The focus should be on the lower rim to draw attention away from the droopy look of the upper part.

To begin, paint the eyelid in a color darker than your skin color up to the crease. If you have medium brown skin, you would use a brown that's darker than your natural color. If you have this kind of eye, you'll see that you don't really have a crease in your eyelid—you have to create one. With your eye closed, use your finger to feel where the natural crease should be. This is the point where you should stop putting color on your lid. To mark that place, use a cotton-tipped applicator and paint some shadow along this edge. Then paint the dark shadow from the rim of the upper eyelid to the imaginary crease.

The color you apply from this imaginary crease up to the eyebrow should be a lighter shade. With medium brown skin you might use beige, caramel, or tan. Be sure to blend these colors so you don't have a sharp line between the dark lid color and the lighter upper skin color. When applying your shadow, always

paint your eye in an upward and outward direction toward the end of your brow so you don't follow the downward arch of the droop.

Now when you open your eye, it will look like it has a natural crease and the droop of the lid will be less noticeable.

TAMING AND SHAPING EYEBROWS

Vanessa Williams's eyebrows complement the natural beauty of the rest of her face. To me, eyebrows are like the final writing on a cake—after the cake is iced, the lettering tops off the job and makes it complete. The eyebrows are the last step that finishes the face and pulls everything together.

THE EYEBROW SHAPE

The shape of your brows depends on the shape of your eyes. The eye and the brow should look balanced.

If you have a very full or wide eye, for example, your brow should be full, not thin.

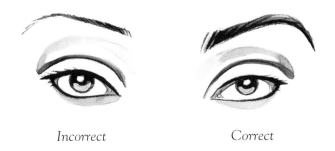

Incorrect   *Correct*

If you have small eyes, you should thin your brows so they don't overwhelm the eye area and detract from the beauty of the eye itself.

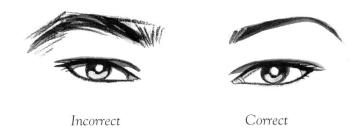

Incorrect   *Correct*

To Tweeze or Not to Tweeze?

Not all women need to shape their eyebrows, but many do. The best way to decide if you should shape your brows is to remember that eyebrows should not close up your face by taking up too much of the eye area or overwhelm the openness and clarity of your eyes. You should consider eyebrow shaping if your brows:

*extend past the outer
ends of your eyes*

*grow toward each other over
the bridge of the nose*

*are bushy, full, or
excessively curly*

There are three ways to shape your eyebrow. You can tweeze, wax, or shave. I recommend tweezing because the results last the longest.

When you begin, follow these steps:

1 *Start tweezing the inner brow above the nose*

2 *Tweeze the brow above the pupil of the eye to create the arch*

3 *Continue tweezing along the brow, pulling each hair out in the direction it is growing*

4 *Make sure all hairs in the tweezed area are removed*

When you buy your tweezer, keep these tips in mind:

- Use the pointed tweezer for removing very fine hairs.

- Use an angled tweezer if you are left-handed.

- Use the flat tweezer for removing excessive hair growth on the brows or for stray hairs you can pull straight out from the chin or upper lip.

EYEBROW COLOR

You can use an eyebrow pencil or colored powder to add color to your eyebrows.

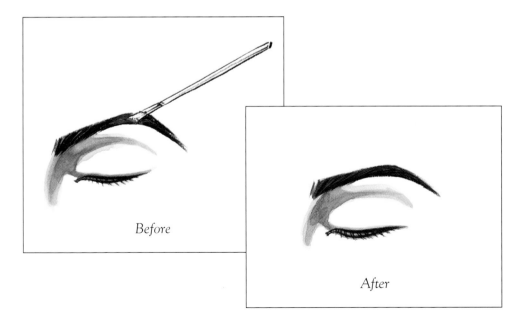

Before

After

You can also fill in thin or spotty brows with your pencil or powder.

Before

After

Bleaching the Brow

If your eyebrows are very dark, you might want to bleach them to lighten their color and soften their effect on the face.

Before

After

COLORING AND
SCULTPING LIPS

Leontyne Price has perfect African-American lips. They are full, shapely, even-colored, and balanced. This isn't to say that all perfect lips fit only one mold—the perfect lips for dark-skinned women come in many different shapes. But there are some common features in the black woman's lips—and if you know how to work with them, your lips can become one of your strongest beauty assets.

The lip shape, texture, and color of African-American women is unique. Just as an artist must consider the size, shape, and texture of his canvas, so must I consider these things in deciding how to apply makeup.

LIP SHAPE

The most important thing to know about lip shape is what *not* to do to shape them. You should not outline your lips with a lip pencil. Lip pencils tend to make a black woman's lips look hard. Your lip already has a definite lip line separating the lip from the skin around it. This defined lip doesn't need more definition. An artist would never use a dark-color outliner on top of an already dark line.

Small Lips

The smaller-shaped lip should always wear darker colors to emphasize and bring out the lip. Stay away from light colors. The color charts in Part IV will show you the lighter lip colors that best match your skin tone.

Incorrect

Correct

Full Lips

If you have full lips, stay away from very strong colors that draw undue attention to the lips. Use a color that complements your skin tone and blends well with dark skin. Use a matte finish lipstick—never use gloss or shiny colors, which further enlarge the look of your lips.

Some black women have a very full bottom lip in comparison to the top lip. If you have this type of lip, you can make the bottom lip look smaller with a camouflage technique by using a matte-type neutral color.

Incorrect

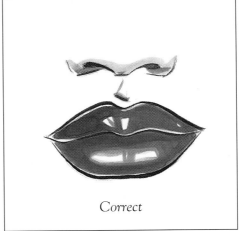

Correct

TEXTURE

African-American women have texture in their lips that Caucasian women don't usually have. The lines in your lips give them depth that can either make your lips look wonderful or unattractive, depending on how you care for them.

In addition to giving your lips a unique appearance, these lines also cause your lips to dry out and crack quickly. Be sure to put a moisturizer on your lips to prevent chapping and cracking before you apply any makeup. In addition, wet glosses or metallics can soften or diminish the textured appearance of your lips. They coat the line crevices so the color of your lipstick doesn't sink so easily into the cracks.

COLOR

Many black women have uneven color in their lips. You can even out the color with a very simple trick that all artists know well—it's called blending. First put a foundation color on the lighter, pinker area of the lip and blend it into the rest of the lip. This foundation should be very close in color to the brown of the rest of the lip and make your lips appear to be all one color. Then apply the lipstick color you want to use on the whole lip.

TIPS TO REMEMBER

So many beautiful African-American women have asked me to "do something with my awful lips." I always tell them that their lips aren't "awful," they're unique. They stand out. Your lips can be your greatest beauty asset if you follow this simple advice:

- Don't use a lip pencil to line your lips.
- Enlarge the look of small lips by wearing dark lipstick colors and avoiding pink and other light colors.
- Minimize the size of exceptionally full lips by using matte finish lipsticks in neutral shades and by avoiding lip gloss.
- Before putting on your lipstick, apply a moisturizer.
- If your lips are not too full, use a gloss over your lipstick to even out the creviced lines.
- Even out any lip discolorations by blending in a dark shade of lipstick that matches the brown of the darker lip color.

CONTOURING
A FULL FACE

The size of a woman's face determines how makeup should be applied. On a full face the job of makeup is to sculpt the shape of the face by bringing out the cheekbones and camouflaging the heavy areas.

CHISELING CHEEKBONES

On a round face, the cheeks need to be contoured to create the space where cheekbones should naturally be. Anything that's dark on the side of the cheek will camouflage the area to make it appear as if it is indented. If you have a full face, follow this technique:

1. Apply your usual foundation. Use one color to serve as a smooth and even base.

2. On both cheeks, use a dark brown pencil to draw a half-inch-thick line going from the bottom tip of the earlobe straight out across the cheek. Stop directly under the center of your eye.

3. Soften that dark line by patting a translucent powder on top of it.

4. Just above the dark line on the cheek, apply a cream beige foundation following the line from the earlobe to the middle of the cheek.

5. Smooth the same cream beige foundation along the line of the jawbone, from the earlobe down to the tip of the chin.

6. Blend in all lines so that none stand apart too sharply from the natural skin color.

There! See how easy it is to sculpt facial contours? The cream foundation is the highlight; it makes the high planes on your face that stand out. The dark colors make the low planes that should almost disappear into darkness.

CONTOURING THE NOSE

If you have enough space between your eyes to place another eye, you have wide-spaced eyes that can make your nose look wider than it really is. You can use a contouring makeup technique to make your eyes look closer together and make your nose look narrower:

1. Using a dark brown pencil, draw a half-inch-thick line down both sides of the nose following the natural line where the nose meets the face.

2. With a lighter pencil or a light highlight pencil, draw a thick line down the middle of the nose.

3. On top of this, blend a cream beige foundation down the center of the nose.

4. Using the same dark pencil you used to contour the cheekbones, draw shadows down the right and left sides of the nose all the way from the tip of the eyebrow to the tip of the nostril.

5. Blend in all makeup so there is no sharp line of separation between colors.

This contouring technique will bring together the area from the inner edge of the eye to the bridge of the nose, and it will give the nose itself a slimmer appearance.

CARING FOR
YOUR SKIN

I t is a pleasure to work on Aretha Franklin's skin because her facial canvas has no bumps, no grooves, no open pores, no changing textures. Applying her foundation is like taking paint and gliding it across a smooth surface. She also knows how to take care of her skin. Before I arrive, I know that she will have prepared her skin for our session by following a careful, but simple, regimen. She begins by washing with a facial soap formulated for her normal skin; then she cleans her pores with a cleansing cream and finishes with the application of her moisturizer. This consistent care and attention gives her a flawless complexion that is a makeup artist's dream.

With the proper attention, I believe that all African-American women can have skin like Aretha's. You have a natural advantage to begin with. Black skin is the envy of all women because of its youthful appearance. It has a sturdy quality that resists lines and wrinkles. It keeps its subtle, soft, and elastic quality far longer than most other skin types. But that doesn't mean it doesn't need special care to keep it clean, smooth, and blemish-free.

EXAMINE YOUR SKIN TYPE

Black women tend to have combination skin. This means they have oily skin in the T-zone area and normal skin on the rest of the face.

You have oil in your T-zone if your nose is often shiny or if you rub a tissue over this area and see oil residue. This oily quality is part of your genetic makeup inherited from your ancestors—it is not caused by eating too many french fries!

Many black women also have open pores in their T-zone. These pores are visibly larger than other pores on your skin. They are the culprit behind the excess oil in your skin, and they also cause other facial problems because the dirt and makeup that your face can collect each day go down into these pores, get stuck, and cause irritation. Oily skin and open pores cause your skin to become unbalanced, which then makes it susceptible to complications such as blackheads, whiteheads, and impurities under the surface of the skin. Proper cleaning can counteract these conditions.

A WEEKLY CLEANSING PLAN

If you have combination or oily skin, give yourself a cleansing mask once a week. This will purge your pores of built-up dirt and impurities left behind by your daily cleansing routine. This is especially important for city dwellers who are exposed to particularly high levels of pollution. Look for a mask that fits your needs. Some are extra-strength formulas for deep cleansing of problem skin; others are milder for normal skin. Also look for masks made specifically for oily skin; they are oil-free and usually contain clay, oat flour, oatmeal, or talc. These products tighten and become hard to the touch after about ten to fifteen minutes. The tightening and drying action will help to absorb excess oils, temporarily counteract enlarged pores, and give a more refined look to the skin.

Masks do a terrific job on oily skin. But if your skin is not oily, don't use them—they are too harsh for normal or dry skin.

A DAILY THREE-STEP CLEANSING PLAN

You should also begin the following daily three-step cleansing routine.

Step One: Wash with a Facial Soap

Soap will remove your makeup and the daily accumulation of dirt quite easily. Choose your soap carefully. Use a facial soap (not a body or deodorant soap!) that is specially formulated for oily, normal, dry, or combination skin.

When cleaning your skin, don't make the mistake of scrubbing hard with soap and a face cloth to get rid of the oil on your face. In many cases you will aggravate the skin, causing it to produce *more* oil. Vigorous scrubbing isn't good for anyone's skin; tugging, rubbing, and pulling weakens the structure and invites lines and wrinkles.

To finish washing, be sure to rinse thoroughly. Rinse and rinse again to remove as much of the soap residue as possible.

Wash your face every morning and before you go to bed.

Step Two: Cleanse with a Facial Cleanser

After your skin is washed with soap, it's not really clean. Take a look at the residue left behind on your shower tiles. That's what remains when you wash something with soap. The same kind of buildup can settle in your open pores after you wash your face. That's why you need to use a cleanser after you use soap. A good facial cleanser penetrates the skin and cleans out any remaining dirt or makeup left behind after washing. Water-based and oil-free gel cleansers are extremely efficient on black skin. Look for products billed as milder, gentler, soap-free, or moisturizing. They rinse well and leave virtually no residue.

Use a cleansing cream twice, daily.

Step Three: Moisturize

Moisturizer, applied in the morning, is a wonderful skin protector. It forms a barrier between your skin and your makeup. It protects against the harshness of weather, it infuses skin with replenishing moisture, and it can contain a sunscreen to protect against harmful sun rays. Whether or not you are wearing makeup, you should be wearing a moisturizer every day, no matter your skin type.

Even if you have combination or oily skin, don't skip this step. The right moisturizer won't make your skin look more oily or shiny. Choose an oil-free, water-based moisturizer formulated not to clog pores; this is usually a lotion that is light and nongreasy. Look for the word "noncomedogenic" on the label. This kind of moisturizer will protect your skin without adding oil.

Unless you have very dry skin (a rarity in black women), you don't need to apply a moisturizer after you cleanse your face at night. And beware of products called night creams. These are useful for dry skin, but most black women have large open pores and oily skin that are aggravated by these creams.

More is not always better—that's the rule in skin care. Beautiful skin comes from these three simple steps. You don't need to wash your face several times a day or apply expensive moisturizers overnight. Simply wash, cleanse, and moisturize to clean and protect the natural beauty of your skin.

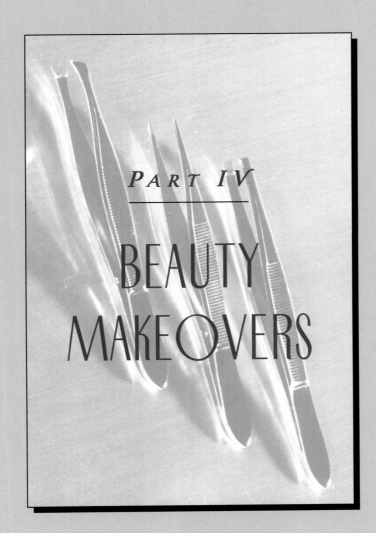

PART IV

BEAUTY
MAKEOVERS

PAINTING THE CANVAS

Before I apply makeup, I look at a woman's face and imagine that I see a brown canvas waiting to be painted. I determine what shade or tone of browness the canvas holds so I can choose colors that will accentuate what's already there.

The canvas of brown skin falls into these three basic categories:

- dark brown
- medium brown
- light brown

These three categories are the basic complexion types found in African-American women, but within each type you'll find a wide variety of tones. Some of these skin tones I call coffee, cinnamon, brown toast, and caramel—all the delicious flavors of dark skin.

The makeovers you'll see in this section give you a good look at the way color is used on each of the three basic color canvases. By comparing the before and after photos, you'll see how correct makeup painting creates illusions that make small eyes look larger, large lips look smaller, uneven skin tones look smooth and even, and unbalanced eyebrows look shapely and well proportioned.

Use these makeovers as a guide in your own exploration of color and its placement. And don't forget to consult the color chart at the end of each makeover—here you'll find the range of colors that best matches your skin tone.

MY MAKEUP PALETTE

Foundation: For these makeovers I used a sponge to apply cream foundations because the sponge and the cream give me more coverage. I also used two different foundation colors on each woman. In the T-zone I put one foundation that is a shade lighter than the natural skin color; then I blended the natural skin color foundation over the entire facial canvas. This technique smooths out the darker tones that African-American women often have in the T-zone area and blends it into the lighter tones on the other areas of the face.

Powder: To set the foundation, I used a pressed powder of different color tints that I apply with a cloth puff. I like pressed powder because it gives me better coverage than translucent powder, and most translucent powders don't have the color tints I like. Pressed powder also softens the face and gives me the look I want.

Blush: On each makeover I used powder blush and applied it with a medium powder brush.

Eye Makeup: I always use powdered eye shadow rather than creams or sticks or any of the other formulations. I like powder because it has a more even consistency and because it absorbs some of the oil from the skin on the lid.

The tools I use to apply eye shadow change depending on the look I'm trying to create. I use a cotton swab applicator to gain a soft look, a sponge applicator to create a smooth and even look, and my fingers when I want heavier coverage.

Mascara: On all of the makeovers, I used black mascara on the upper lashes only. This keeps the attention away from the area below the eye, where many flaws like bags, circles, and wrinkles often appear.

Lipstick: I colored the lips in each of these makeovers with lipstick from a tube that's applied with a brush.

MAKEOVER ONE: DARK SKIN

STEP ONE: FOUNDATION

This dark skin canvas had oily skin, so I did not use a moisturizer before makeup application.

Using the double foundation technique, I applied a lighter foundation (oil-free) in the T-zone and then blended over it a foundation that matches the natural skin color.

Powder: On this dark brown skin, I applied a dark brown pressed powder.

STEP TWO: BLUSH

I used a very simple blush application by blending in a rose blush right in the center of the cheek.

STEP THREE: EYES

Because these eyes are small, I wanted to apply makeup that would make them appear larger. I rimmed the eye with a metallic burgundy eye shadow, which tends to open up the eye. From the eyebrow to the crease of the eye I used a metallic soft rose using a sponge eye-makeup applicator to achieve an even and smooth application.

Eyebrows: After shaping the brows with tweezers to arch the brow to match the shape of the eye, I filled in the color with a dark brown eyebrow pencil.

STEP FOUR: LIPS

These lips are colored with a double lipstick color. First I placed a burgundy red on the lips to give bright color to the entire mouth. Then on the upper lip, I blended in a matted soft rose color. On the bottom lip, right in the center, I blended a frosted rose lip color. This double color technique is used to make this small lip look a little fuller.

YOUR PERSONAL COLOR CHART FOR DARK SKIN

This color chart is your guide to makeup selection. Choose the colors that will complement your skin tone.

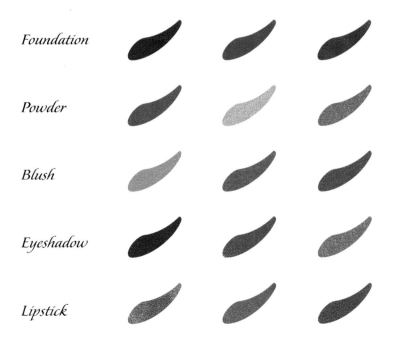

Foundation

Powder

Blush

Eyeshadow

Lipstick

MAKEOVER TWO: MEDIUM SKIN

This medium brown face had combination skin (oily in the T-zone and dry on the outer areas). Before applying foundation I used a combination skin moisturizer to prepare the canvas.

Using the double foundation technique, I applied a foundation in the T-zone one shade lighter than this medium brown skin. Over that I blended in a foundation that matches the natural skin color.

Powder: On this medium brown skin, I applied a golden pressed powder with a cloth puff.

STEP TWO: BLUSH

I used a simple application of a medium brown blush placed right in the center of the cheek.

STEP THREE: EYES

These round eyes are quite attractive, but I wanted to give them a bit more of an elongated appearance. To do this, I used a dark brown liquid liner along the upper lashes, and I put a dark brown eye shadow on the lid and extended it up and out toward the tip of the eyebrow. From the crease of the eye to the eyebrow I painted a beige shadow. I applied the shadow with a cotton-tipped applicator because this tip gives a very soft look. Along the lower lashes, I used a tan eye shadow.

Eyebrows: After shaping these brows with tweezers to give them a natural arch, I used a light brown pencil to fill the body of the brow.

STEP FOUR: LIPS

These lips are medium sized and nicely shaped. I accented their natural beauty by painting them with a dark shade of brown. Then I painted a wet gloss over the bottom lip to fill in and soften some of the texture in the lip.

YOUR PERSONAL COLOR CHART FOR MEDIUM SKIN

This color chart is your guide to makeup selection. Choose the colors that will complement your skin tone.

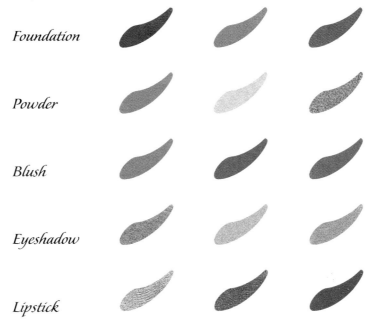

Foundation

Powder

Blush

Eyeshadow

Lipstick

MAKEOVER THREE: LIGHT SKIN

STEP ONE: FOUNDATION

This light skin was very dry, so before applying the foundation, I used a moisturizer to make the skin more supple and receptive to the makeup.

Using the double foundation technique, I applied a lighter foundation in the T-zone and then over that I blended a foundation color that matches the natural skin color.

Powder: The foundation on this light skin was set with a pressed powder with a yellowish tint applied with a cloth puff.

STEP TWO: BLUSH

On this light skin, I used a medium coral blush blended in the center of the cheek.

STEP THREE: EYES

These eyes are deep-set—the most naturally perfect type of eye. The shape of the deep-set eye makes its own shadow naturally because of the perfect placement of the crease in the lid. Using my finger, I applied a light coral eye shadow on the lid, being careful not to get any in the crease. I rimmed this eye with medium rust eye shadow and used a bone shadow beneath the eyebrow.

Eyebrows: Many light-skinned women tend to have very dark brows. After tweezing and shaping these eyebrows, I used a bleaching cream to lighten them

and soften the entire look. This also helped match the color of the brows to the color of the hair. To fill in the gaps, I used a dark blond pencil.

STEP FOUR: LIPS

These full lips need only one color in a darker tone. I chose a medium rust color.

YOUR PERSONAL COLOR CHART FOR LIGHT SKIN

This color chart is your guide to makeup selection. Choose the colors that will complement your skin tone.

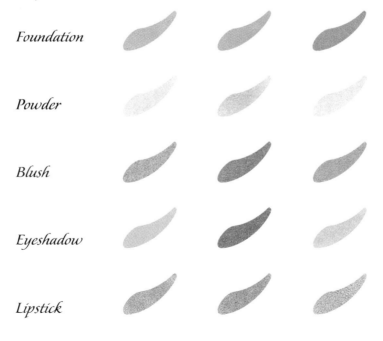

Foundation

Powder

Blush

Eyeshadow

Lipstick

CLIENT LIST

WOMEN

Aaliyah (vocalist)

Karen Alexander (model-actor)

Mary Alice (actor)

Debbie Allen (vocalist-actor-choreographer)

Maya Angelou (author-actor)

Aria (actor)

Trisha Arnold (actor)

Ethel Aylers (actor)

Cynthia Bailey (model-actor)

Anita Baker (vocalist)

Halle Berry (actor-model)

Vanessa Bell Armstrong (vocalist)

Regina Belle (vocalist)

Garcelle Beauvais (model-actor)

Tracy Bingham (actor)

Billie Blair (model)

Lisa Bonet (actor)

Kersti Bowser (model)

Brandy (vocalist-actor)

Julie Brown (actor–TV host)

Jolie Burrell (model-entrepreneur)

Michele Burton (model)

Vanessa Bell Calloway (actor)

Maia Campbell (actor)

Naomi Campbell (model-author)

Jean Carnes (vocalist)

Diahann Carroll (vocalist-actor)

Betty Carter (jazz vocalist)

Nell Carter (vocalist-actor)

Pat Cleveland (model)

Co Co (model)

Natalie Cole (vocalist-actor)

Dr. Johnnetta B. Cole (president, Spelman College)

Celia Cruz (vocalist-actor)

Dominique Dawes (Olympic gymnast)

Ruby Dee (actor)

Carman de Lavallade (dancer-actor)

Suzanne de Passe (producer)

Peggy Dillard (model-entrepreneur)

En Vogue (vocal group)

Faith Evans (vocalist)

Kim Fields (actor)

Roberta Flack (vocalist)

Aretha Franklin (vocalist)

Zina Garrison (tennis player)

Marla Gibbs (actor)

Bethann Hardison (model-actor)

Jackee Harry (actor)

Lalah Hathaway (vocalist)

Shari Headley (model-actor)

Taral Hicks (vocalist-actor)

Lauren Hill (vocalist-actor)

Jennifer Holliday (vocalist)

Whitney Houston (vocalist-actor)

Mikki Howard (vocalist)

Bobby Humphrey (jazz musician)

Phyllis Hyman (vocalist)

Iman (model-actor)

Janet Jackson (vocalist)

Judith Jamison (dancer–artistic director, Alvin Ailey American Dance Theater)

Beverly Johnson (model-actor)

Linda Rice Johnson (president, Fashion Fair Cosmetics)

Shelia Johnson (model-actor)

Caroline R. Jones (publicist)

Florence Griffith-Joyner (track and field Olympic athlete)

Chaka Khan (vocalist)

Waneda Jordan (author)

Jackie Joyner-Kersee (track and field Olympic athlete)

Jane Kennedy (actor)

Gayle King (talk show host)

Regina King (actor)

Patti LaBelle (vocalist)

Janet Langheart (journalist)

Queen Latifah (actor-vocalist)

Abbey Lincoln (actor-vocalist-songwriter)

Gloria Lynne (vocalist)

Magic (designer-model)

Jewel Jackson McCabe (president, Coalition of 100 Black Women)

Maria McDonald (model-actor)

Terry McMillan (author)

Lori McNeil (tennis player)

Michael Michele (actor)

Stephanie Mills (vocalist-actor)

Melba Moore (vocalist-actor)

Debbi Morgan (actor)

Meli-sa Morgan (vocalist)

Mounia (model)

Gail O'Neil (model)

Peaches and Herb (vocal group)

Pebbles (vocalist)

Sheryl Lee Ralph (actor)

Theresa Randal (actor)

Phylicia Rashad (actor-vocalist)

Roshumba (actor-model)

Holly Robertson (actor)

Diana Ross (vocalist-actor)

Tracy Ross (actor-model)

Roz Ryan (vocalist-actor)

Attallah Shabazz (author)

Ntozake Shange (author)

Coreen Simpson (designer-photographer)

Valerie Simpson (vocalist-producer)

Naomi Sims (model)

Sister Sledge (vocal group)

Barbara Smith (model-author-restaurant owner)

Tookie Smith (model-actor)

Dakota Staton (vocalist)

Sarah Stavrou (model-actor)

Phyllis Yvonne Stickney (actor)

Sybil (vocalist)

Tawaffa (vocalist)

Mikki Taylor (beauty editor)

Susan L. Taylor (author-editor)

Gay Thomas (model-actor)

Cicely Tyson (actor)

Vanity (actress)

Louise Vyent (model)

Alice Walker (author)

Wanake (model)

Pauletta Washington (vocalist-actor)

Jody Watley (vocalist)

Faye Wattleton (former president,
  Planned Parenthood)

Veronica Webb (model)

Karyn White (vocalist)

Cinda Williams (actor)

Deniece Williams (vocalist)

Vanessa Williams (actor-vocalist)

Cassandra Wilson (jazz vocalist)

Nancy Wilson (vocalist)

MEN

Mohammed Ali (former world-champion
  boxer)

Baby Face (songwriter-vocalist-producer)

Mark Breland (boxer)

Ed Bradley (broadcast journalist)

Bobby Brown (vocalist)

Cameo (vocal group)

Jimmy Cliff (jazz musician)

Sean "Puffy" Combs (vocalist-producer)

Miles Davis (musician)

Ossie Davis (actor)

Morris Day (vocalist)

El de Barge (vocalist)

Giancarlo Esposito (actor)

Fourth M.D. (vocal group)

Ron Glass (actor)

Stedman Graham (publicist)

Herbie Hancock (musician)

Edward Hawkins (gospel vocalist)

Gregory Hines (actor-dancer)

Freddie Jackson (vocalist)

Reverend Jesse Jackson (politician)

Michael Jackson (vocalist)

James Earl Jones (actor)

Michael Jordon (basketball player)

Ben Lawson (model)

Spike Lee (actor-director)

Wynton Marsalis (jazz musician)

Kweisi Mfume (director, NAACP)

Eddie Murphy (actor-comic)

Ken Norton (boxer)

Ahmad Rashad (sportscaster)

Ray Goodman & Brown (vocal group)

Howard Rollins (actor)

Bobby Short (vocalist)

Rashid Silvera (educator-model)

Ty Spears (model-entrepreneur)

Michael Spinks (boxer)

Al B. Sure (vocalist-producer)

Robert Townsend (actor-director)

Mike Tyson (boxer)

Luther Vandross (vocalist)

Mario Van Peebles (actor)

Denzel Washington (actor)

Grover Washington Jr. (musician)

Renauld White (actor-model)

Billy Dee Williams (actor)

BeBe Winans (vocalist)

Bobby Womack (vocalist)

Photographic Credits

p. ii Anthony Barboza; p. vi Tom Wool; p. x A. Buckmaster; p. xiii Marili Forastieri; p. xv Kevin McDonald; p. 3 Anthony Barboza; p. 4 Courtesy of the Wells Photo Collection; p. 6 Courtesty of the Wells Photo Collection; p. 7 Courtesy of the Wells Photo Collection; p. 8 (all) Courtesy of the Wells Photo Collection; p. 9 Courtesy of the Wells Photo Collection; p. 10 Theo, Courtesy of *Bride's* magazine; p. 13 Hank Londener; p. 14 (right) A. Buckmaster, (left) Debra Feingold; p. 15 Anthony Barboza; p. 16 (top) Bill Wylie, (bottom) Andrea Alberts; p. 17 Bernard Vidal; p. 19 Anthony Barboza; p. 20 Jack Mitchell; p. 22 Jack Mitchell; p. 24 Jack Mitchell; p. 25 Jack Mitchell; p. 27 Francesco Scavullo; p. 28 Gerard Gentil; p. 32 (all) Gerard Gentil; p. 34 Knut Bry; p. 36 Bonoit, Courtesy of *Essence* magazine; p. 39 Anthony Barboza; p. 41 Courtesy of the Wells Photo Collection; p. 42 Bob Sacha, Courtesy of *Life* magazine; p. 45 Bob Sacha; p. 47 Courtesy of the Wells Photo Collection; p. 48 A. Buckmaster, Courtesy of *Essence* magazine; p. 49 A. Buckmaster; p. 50 Alen MacWeeney; p. 54 Courtesy of the Wells Photo Collection; p. 56 A. Buckmaster, Courtesy of *Esssence* magazine; p. 59 Anthony Barboza; p. 60 Courtesy of the Wells Photo Collection; p. 62 A. Buckmaster; p. 65 A. Buckmaster; p. 66 A. Buckmaster, Courtesy of *Essence* magazine; p. 68 A. Buckmaster; p. 69 Courtesy of the Wells Photo Collection; p. 70 Jacques Malignon, Courtesy of *Essence* magazine; p. 73 Jacques Malignon; p. 75 Jacques Malignon; p. 78 Francesco Scavullo; p. 80 Alberto Tolot; p. 82 Ron Slenzak; p. 83 Tim Defrisco; p. 84 Alberto Tolot; p. 85 Matthew Jordon Smith; p. 87 Matthew Jordon Smith, Courtesy of *Essence* magazine; p. 88 Skrebneski; p. 89 Skrebneski; p. 90 Dwight Carter; p. 91 Kip Meyer, Courtesy of *Essence* magazine; p. 92 Peter Mulder; p. 94 A. Buckmaster; p. 96 Courtesy of the Wells Photo Collection; p. 97 Bob Kiss, Courtesy of *Essence* magazine; p. 98 A. Buckmaster, Courtesy of *Essence* magazine; p. 99 (all) Bob Kiss; p. 100 Anthony Barboza (makeup by Milagros, hair by Marc Daniels); p. 106 Michael Wong; p. 109 Max Vadukul; p. 110 Max Vadukul; p. 111 Martaez Cyars; p. 112 Charlie Pizzarello; p. 115 Charlie Pizzarello, Courtesy of *Essence* magazine; p. 116 Charlie Pizzarello; p. 117 Charlie Pizzarello; p. 118 Courtesy of the Wells Photo Collection; p. 120 Brad Hitz; p. 123 Brad Hitz; p. 125 Brad Hitz; p. 126 (top) Sean A. Burrowes, (bottom) Bernard Vidal; p. 128 (top) John Beckett, (bottom) Ron Slenzak; p. 131 Anthony Barboza; p. 132 John Penden; p. 140 Tom Wool; p. 146 Nesti; p. 152 A. Buckmaster; p. 158 Gerard Gentil; p. 163 Anthony Barboza; p. 165 Anthony Barboza, p. 166 (all) Phyllis Cuington; p. 169 A. Buckmaster; p. 170 Tom Wool; p. 173 Matthew Jordan Smith; p. 177 Matthew Jordan Smith; p. 181 Matthew Jordan Smith; p. 183 Anthony Barboza; p. 185 Anthony Barboza; p. 186 Courtesy of *Essence* magazine (from left to right), *top row:* Paul Lange, Terry Wier, Frank Schramm, Bob Kiss, Bob Kiss, Bob Kiss; *second row:* Tim White, Andrea Alberts, Matthew Rolston, Gerard Gentil, Jacques Malignon, Phyllis Cuington; *third row:* Bob Kiss, Phyllis Cuington, Bill Wylie, Bill Wylie, Bill Wyllie, Andrea Alberts; *fourth row:* A. Buckmaster, A. Buckmaster, A. Buckmaster, A. Buckmaster, Tom Wool, Dwight Carter; *fifth row:* Bonoit, Tom Wool, Phyllis Cuington, Bonoit, Marili Forastieri, Matthew Jordan Smith

CYNTHIA BAILEY

Sarah Sta

Wanakee